Charles Daney . Boubacar Seck . Bruno Boidron
Louise Gabriel .

Translated by
Photography by

The *Place de la Bourse* and its Water Mirror

© ELYTIS 2009
51, avenue Jeanne d'Arc 33000 BORDEAUX
www.elytis-edition.com
ISBN : 978-2-35639-023-3

A Short Break in Bordeaux

Marie-Laure Hubert-Nasser . Michel Suffran .
Kevin Desmond . Stéphanie Baudry .

Susan Brown
Philippe Roy

ELYTIS

UNIVERSAL AND INEFFABLE, Bordeaux evokes the name of our famous *vignoble* in every language. United within the same appellation, both the wine and the city travel the world together offering sheer body and soul goodness. "A Short Break in Bordeaux" partakes in the radiance of our region as it reveals appealing territorial diversity like an invitation to stay.

This superb book on Bordeaux is aimed at every English speaking person desirous to discover the wealth of our architectural, historical, literary and gastronomic heritage; truly, the work of people. Indeed, since its birth Bordeaux never ceased to welcome men and women who contributed to create a unique spirit, identity and quality of life. While being a City of Culture, Bordeaux is also young and full of life, quite a rare combination. The Bordeaux World Heritage site is the largest urban entity to be so honored.

Around the time *Aliénor d'Aquitaine* wedded *Henri Plantagenêt* our region would produce a *claret* much appreciated by the English. I wish similar success to this book! I welcome such a great editorial initiative and invite all to journey along its pages.

ALAIN JUPPÉ
MAYOR OF BORDEAUX

Les vins de Bordeaux [1]

subtle Alchemy of Water and Wine

by . Bruno . Boidron

BORDEAUX is a Port City created by foreigners for foreigners, an exchange place, a cosmopolitan city bustling with merchants from the world over. With such a wealth of flavors, with such a spirit of seduction, how could Bordeaux Wines not be the greatest in the world?

To discover them, one must roam around traveling the four seasons to fully grasp what it takes to maintain a vineyard, to understand the difference between vintages and the sheer complexity of wines…

Each vintage (and there are near seven thousand of them) being particular, it is quite impossible to know everything about Bordelaise wines. A good acquaintance with *appellations* (53), and a discovery itinerary can nonetheless deliver a key into the Bordeaux Wines world.

A world naturally divided into three large geographical zones. The left banks of the Garonne and then of the Gironde rivers, the right banks of the Dordogne and the Gironde rivers, and lastly *l'Entre-deux-Mers* (between two seas) nestled in between the first two regions. This division is not merely geographical. The natural frontiers thus defined truly impacted the minds. Montesquieu hailed from the left banks, Montaigne from the right. Mauriac, who settled in Malagar (*Entre-deux-Mers*), would gaze

➡ *Vine plant*

longingly towards the Jacobin right banks yet was held back still by the left bank spirit. Even if the second half of the Twentieth Century deeply changed many things, the past cannot be erased so easily…

Roaming through vineyards, one cannot but be moved by how deeply attached the men and women are to their land, to their wines. Some remained *Gascon* and grumpy. You will be made welcome on the condition, as with every thing, that you show a minimum of courtesy. One must never forget that vine culture is a patience game. Plantations are to last 30 to 40 years, grapes are harvested only once every year, and winegrowers like to take time for reflection. He who understands these facts might, in turn, take the necessary time to appreciate, and perhaps even love, this special world.

DISCOVERING THE BORDEAUX VINEYARDS

Amateurs must know that anywhere in the Gironde region, one can find *AOC* [2] productions of Bordeaux and Bordeaux Superior. The Bordeaux *appellation* embraces the entire department entity. Bordeaux and Bordeaux Superior *appellations* are the first of the French *AOC* in terms of

volume and surface. Among others, the *Châteaux Thieulet, Bonnet…* or again *Château Parenchère*, the vines of which are situated at the frontier of the Gironde region, a stone's throw from the Dordogne and the *Lot et Garonne*.

The left banks are those of Bordeaux itself, of the *Girondin* spirit, of independence and of investors. The latter's freedom in addition to local practices gave birth in 1855 to a *Gironde* wine classification, which established the banks as a whole. The *Premiers Crus* [3] thus obtained are renowned, *Margaux, Latour, Lafite, Mouton, Haut-Brion, Yquem…*

A great journey through the Bordelaise vineyards must begin in the *Médoc* region and be water bound. One must indeed cross *Cordouan*, where many exchanges take place, and put into the *Port du Verdon*. From the *Pointe de Grave* [4] one can thus reach the *Sauternais* region without yet ever leaving the banks.

The *Médoc* is a triangular peninsula. On the east side, the vines flank the rivers (Gironde & Garonne), stretching from the *Pointe de Grave* as far as the North-Western side of Bordeaux. Out west, the forests and the *Lande* form a luxuriant screen right into the Atlantic Ocean. The *Médocain* vineyard is thus nestled between two very large water masses, namely the Ocean and the Estuary which attenuate climatic excesses. Temperature differences are lesser and springtime frost milder than elsewhere.

The vines are mainly implanted in gravelly land. Due to their permeability, they are particularly well-suited to the production of quality wines. There, *Cabernet* is king. Undoubtedly, vineyard division in this region is the wisest around. Eight *appellations* coexist, two "regional" ones: *Médoc and Haut-Médoc*, and six "communal" ones: *Saint-Estèphe,*

Pauillac, Saint-Julien, Moulis, Listrac and *Margaux*. The lands of the latter are jealously guarded by the most sought-after vintages such as *Marbuzet, Cos, Lynch-Bages,* the *Léoville* (of which the first-rank *Las Cases*), and many others worth discovering…

The *Graves,* inside and south of the city, long before the *Médoc,* acquired their reputation during the Middle Ages.

➡ *Vineyards from the Médoc region*

Bordeaux and its Wines

Charente-Maritime

Charente

Dordogne

Landes

Lot-et-Garonne

Côtes et Premières Côtes de Blaye

Côtes de Bourg

Graves-de-Vayres

Canon-Fronsac

Fronsac

Lalande-de-Pomerol

Pomerol

Bordeaux et Bordeaux Supérieur

Lussac-Saint-Émilion

Montagne-Saint-Émilion

Bordeaux-Côtes de Francs

Saint-Georges-Saint-Émilion

Puisseguin-Saint-Émilion

Côtes de Castillon

Saint-Émilion

Sainte-Foy-Bordeaux Bordeaux et Bordeaux Supérieur

Entre-Deux-Mers Bordeaux et Bordeaux Supérieur

Bordeaux Haut-Benauge et Entre-Deux-Mers-Haut-Benauge

Côtes de Bordeaux-Saint-Macaire

Bordeaux et Bordeaux Supérieur

LESPARRE-MÉDOC

Médoc

Saint-Estèphe

Pauillac

Saint-Julien

Haut-Médoc

Listrac-Médoc

Moulis

Margaux

Haut-Médoc

BORDEAUX

Premières Côtes de Bordeaux

Pessac-Léognan

Premières Côtes de Bordeaux et Cadillac

Graves et Graves Supérieures

Cérons et Graves

Barsac

Loupiac

Sainte-Croix-du-Mont

Sauternes

BLAYE

LIBOURNE

LANGON

0   10 km

N

BORDEAUX

NSEIL INTERPROFESSIONNEL DU VIN DE BORDEAUX

1, cours du XXX Juillet 33075 Bordeaux Cedex France
Tél. 33 (0)5 56 00 22 66 - Fax 33 (0)5 56 00 22 82
civb@vins-bordeaux.fr - www.bordeaux.com

Mai 2006

Great names are linked to this historic region: the *Prince Noir* [5] owned a hunting domain in *Léognan*, Montesquieu, winemaker and philosopher, lived at the *La Brède* and also the *Rochemorin* castles. Some vintages are *classés* [6] there, evoking prestigious names: the *Château Haut-Brion (classé 1er cru* [7] in 1855), property of His Highness the Prince of Luxembourg, but also *Pape Clément* in *Pessac*, created in 1300 by *Bertrand de Goth* who was elected Pope under the name of *Clément V* in 1305. One could also mention many others such as *Latour Martillac, Haut-Bailly*… Nearly all are located in the area of the *Pessac-Léognan appellation*. After having visited a few vintages from this region, amateurs will grasp the full meaning of this sentence by Jean Kressmann: *"There is more history than geography inside a bottle of wine"*. Indeed, Bordeaux carved her way into History as well as into a universal *art de vivre* [8].

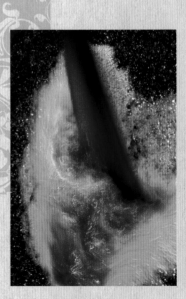

➡ Harvesting Time…

The Lafaurie Peyraguey Castle

The barrel wine storehouse of the Fargues Castle

Last stop on the left banks: the *Sauternais*. The common denominator for the wines in this region is a river: the *Ciron*. It is located near the *Sauternes* communes *Bommes, Preignac, Fargues* and *Barsac* and makes for a particular climate, highly favorable to noble decay. These *liquoreux* wines are a gorgeous antique gold shade, they are sweet, full-bodied and quietly powerful with an exceptional toasty character.

Their aromas evoke citrus fruit, acacia, and apricot together in a complex symphony. Ideal *liquoreux* wines, they are, as a poet once said, a "perfect extravaganza". With passing years they grow unctuous, racy and develop a very particular body. They can also be enjoyed in their prime youth for their fruity and zesty flavor. *D'Yquem* remains a prince among these wines.

Between the *Dordogne* and the *Garonne* reigns the aptly-named *Entre-deux-Mers.* Coast after coast, the *appellation* owns a great and magnificent historical, archeological and monumental patrimony including megalithic sites, windmills,

pigeon-houses, churches, abbeys, powerful plazas and old towns. Given the stretch of this region, soils are quite varied. Three main *appellations* stand out, the *AOC Entre-deux-Mers,* the *Côtes de Bordeaux,* and of course the *Bordeaux* and *Bordeaux Superior.*

In *Saint-Emilion*

As renowned for her architecture as for her wine excellence, *Saint-Emilion* is an original medieval town, and is one of the UNESCO World Heritage Sites.

Vines were implanted in this land as early as on the other banks, but the resulting wines were not acknowledged until the end of the 19th Century. In addition to the lack of an efficient trade, when Jefferson came to visit the region at the end of the 18th Century the *Merlot,* most appropriate *cépage* [9] to *Saint-Emilion*'s argillaceous soils, was not known yet. It had to wait until around 1830 before being widely used.

Over 500 vintages can claim two *AOCs,* namely *Saint-Emilion* and *Saint-Emilion Grand Cru* (the latter having stricter production and agreement conditions than the former).

Grand Cru Classé and *Premier Grand Cru Classé* are terms exclusively reserved for vineyards which have been officially ranked and recognized, and for the resulting wines which meet the required production conditions for the *"Saint-Emilion Grand Cru"* appellation. The two most renowned, namely *Ausone* and *Cheval-Blanc* are much sought-after nectars throughout the world.

The Pape-Clément Castle

The Filhot Castle

The Cantenac Brown Castle

The Smith Haut Lafitte Castle

➡ *The Margaux Castle*

➡ *The Yquem Castle*

➡ *The Laroque Castle*

➡ *The Pichon Longueville Castle*

The first time I met Jean-Michel Cazes, we had a drink together at home, on the patio, on a warm summer afternoon.

I met a man gifted for life, extremely attentive to all and everything around him, naturally charming, but of whom I had not the true measure yet! To pursue his father André's works, he worked relentlessly, skillfully mixing a modern approach with a deep respect for what had been done before him. It was on a nice early autumn afternoon at the terrace of his Lavinal café that I really discovered the man. I must say that the Bages village plaza which he is restoring little by little bears his love for his parents' land, and for the generations to come whose future he also prepares. Andréa, his sweet grandmother, comes back to life at the Baba where croissants are as divine as bread, the Café Brasserie Lavinal was named after his mother's maiden name to honor traditional cuisine and yesteryear's flavors, and the Bages' Bazaar offers a wide array of wine fineries, from indispensable ustensils to degustation to again bottles from his "chateaux" delicately lain in eponymous crates. Books on wine and food, true "art of living" guides chosen by one of his daughters, are plentiful and remarkable in quality and originality! Take a stroll around the plaza and as you set off back towards Lynch-Bages or towards his starred restaurant Cordeillan-Bages and, through a slightly ajar wine storehouse

Jean-Michel Cazes

BAGES' BAZAAR

door, you might catch a glimpse of the degustation room where lovers of his wine escape time to savor the wine, attentive to the lady guides' sharpened commentaries. Jean-Michel Cazes captivated more than one wine amateur and convinced more than one expert. The French astronaut Patrick Baudry made a point – and more so, a pleasure – of bringing a Lynch-Bages 1975 on-board the Discovery shuttle, the first earthly wine to travel in space! Linked to his roots, anchored in them like vine in earth, he nonetheless remains on the cutting edge of wine art, such as his creation of the Bages Bordeaux Wine School. Today his son Jean-Charles succeeds him with verve and in true respect for his father's work, never forgetting for one moment that this man simply always is one – excellent – idea ahead of others to give his wine and his village the necessary enterprising spirit for both creativity and longevity. Spending a few hours in Bages unveils what Jean-Michel Cazes likes most in the world; and if you spot in the vineyards a solid silhouette forthrightly advancing and looking ahead, eyes slightly to the

sky, you will have seen the owner of the lands. Later recollecting the moment, you will not manage to separate his body from his land, as they are indivisible indeed. The vineyards of magical Pauillac will reappear before your eyes as you open one of the Lynch-Bages bottles you could not resist bringing back with you, liberating a powerful wine with a stupefying architecture, solid as its owners, in one word: sublime!

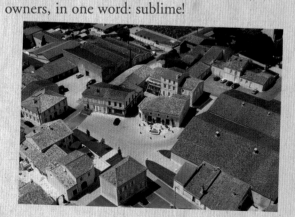

➡ *The Bages hamlet*

But sometimes no particular ranking is required to establish an *AOC*. *Pomerol* is a true example of this: during the 12th Century, the powerful Knights of St-John-of-Jerusalem founded their first Commandery in the region. There, they built their manor, a hospital and a church. As early as 1900, *Pomerol* winemakers formed a syndicate to defend their *appellation*, with in particular the aim to prevent neighboring communes from excessively stamping their barrels in the name of their *AOC*.

Pétrus is the most renowned of these wines, and around forty other *crus* should not be missed, such as *Bourgneuf Vayron*.

in hand along roads and paths, free from any preconceived thought.

➡ *The barrel wine storehouse of the Lafite Rothschild Castle*

Bordeaux is rich with diversity, with such names as *Lalande-de-Pomerol* (which neighbors the above-mentioned), the *AOC Montagne-Saint-Emilion, Saint-Georges Saint-Emilion, Lussac-Saint-Emilion,* and *Puisseguin Saint-Emilion.* Then the *Côtes de Bordeaux* from the region, the *Côtes de Castillon, Côtes de Francs, Côtes de Blaye,* and *Côtes de Bourg* withstanding still, and we would indeed need many more pages yet to fully grasp the immense Bordeaux wine wealth…

Indeed, in Bordeaux, nature showed her generous side and composed a wonderful symphony… Earth, lands, vines, sun, ocean gentleness belong to each and everyone to discover and sublimate, traveling glass

➡ *The wine storehouses of the Old Certan Castle*

➡ *The underground barrel wine storehouse of the Gruaud Larose Castle*

Henri Duboscq

Henri, Hugues and Bruno Duboscq, a unique destiny spanning over two generations. It all began when Henri's father Hervé, a shepherd from the Gers region, became winemaker out of love for his land and her vines. A love shared by the Duboscq father, children and grandchildren. Even Liliane, Henri's wife, lovingly cultivates roses in this land. Haut-Marbuzet, a great terroir, a unique method of new barrels, direct sales and countless visits... Henri is a winemaker who year after year creates a poetic wine, full of panache like his owner, himself a gifted orator. All the ingredients to a marvel among the Médoc crus! Dégustation time thus becomes an exceptional moment, charming and voluptuous... Henri might even share with you some of the secrets which made his wine a success story, in a conversation roaming from culture to poetry, along the lines of wine and word generosity!

➡ *Henri Duboscq, owner of the Haut-Marbuzet Castle*

CÉPAGES (GRAPE VARIETIES)

Most cépages found in the Bordelaise region are for red wine: the Cabernet Franc, the Cabernet Sauvignon, the Malbec and the Merlot Noir. For the whites, the main ones are the Muscadelle, the Sauvignon and the Semillon.

AROMAS AND BOUQUETS

Before being bottled, Bordeaux wines are characterized, for the whites, by the presence of vegetal aromas mainly from flowers, and red fruit (blackcurrants, cherries, strawberries, raspberries) for the reds.

Once bottled, a transformation takes place where various aromas appear: they can be wooden, animal (leather) or vegetal (resin, mushrooms, undergrowth etc). These are called "bouquets".

BARRIQUES (BARRELS)

Bordelaise barriques hold 225 liters each. Two barriques make a pipe (450 liters) and two pipes a larger barrel called a tonneau (900 liters). It used to be the main conditioning for transportation. Carpenters would either make barriques, tonneaux and pipes as bushels or other dry-matter containers. The barriques were also used as liquid capacity measuring units.

A Sculpture by Zadkine representing François Mauriac

➥ The Malagar *Estate*

Writers in Bordeaux

by . Michel . Suffran

BORDEAUX… why such a strange spelling? The Latin used to say *Burdigala, Burdeu* in Gascon… – both in the singular tense. So what can this "x" ending possibly mean, if not the incongruous fact that there has never been only one Bordeaux but several, an entangled multitude, superposed, overlapped, amalgamated into one another? And sometimes even cancelled by each other.

Why then should Bordeaux be unique?

And what remains of the antique Burdigala, apart from the dismantled ruins of the "Palais Gallien [10]"? What does the medieval *Burdeu* hand us down apart from the *Grosse Cloche*'s [11] belfry and a few half-timbering houses in the *La Rousselle* district ? An entire era spanning over more than a millennium has been swallowed beneath this yellow stone slab, beautifully worked, which had been imposed by the "Grands Intendants [12]" during the 18th Century. Remember Baudelaire's *Lamento* : "The form of a city changes faster, alas, than the human heart [13]…" The form, undoubtedly. But what of the heart, the soul? In this sense, one can wonder if the true builders of a city, more so even than architects and planners, were not the stubborn who sensed her very spirit, celebrated her true soul – in other words, her writers, those who managed to capture and translate beyond metamorphoses what Camille Jullian, visionary historian,

so beautifully called "the voice of the sovereign person called Bordeaux City".

In the 4th Century, a poet named Ausone – an erudite humanist who was also Prefect of Gaul – drew a portrait full of fervour and vitality which in parts took on the enthusiasm of an ode to love, not to say a sacred song:

➨ *The Ruins of the Gallien Palace*

➡ *The* Saint-Projet *district*

"I was born in Burdigala where the sky
is soft and mild, the spring long and
the winter brief, the hills wooden.
Its river simmers, imitating the ocean's
ebb tide… I admire the beauteous
architectural arrangement of houses,
of large plazas, of open porticos at the
street ends… I salute you, fountain
from unknown source, saint, eternal,
crystalline, murmuring, limpid,
shaded. I salute you, city genius,
fountain called Divona by the Celtic
tongue and raised to Divinity rank…
between Rome and Burdigala, which
is triumphant? Burdigala has my love,
Rome my veneration. Here my cradle,
there my curule chair. [14]"

What could one add to such a
passionate declaration?
The shining city surrounded by the
Alyscamps [15] and opened onto the
sensitive universe would dwindle little
by little over the course of invasions
and menaces, like a nut dried up inside
its hard-shell of rugged walls.
Montaigne, who yet was the city's

mayor, elected by plebiscite on two
accounts between 1581 and 1585, did
not, in his *Essais*, indulge the slightest
line to testify of this rough labyrinth.

Both a precursor and a man of his
time, he embodied, heart and soul,
the dark and still medieval Bordeaux
which yet started, here and there, with
the carving of a baluster, to be nudged
by the golden wing of the Renaissance.
He who was chosen to be "Premier
Magistrat [16]" became the untiring passerby in this maze of alleys and impasses.
With his legendary clairvoyance, he
declared playfully: "Everyone can see me
in my book, and see my book in
myself".
Indeed Montaigne did not describe
himself, rather he wrote himself.

He was first and foremost the *passerby* whom he profiled in this deeply moving phrase: "I do not depict the being, I depict the passing". Put in other words, the sweeping movement, the uplifting breath, the hauling abyss.

Contradistinct in method as in design, the Baron de Montesquieu Charles-Louis de Secondat appeared at the dawn of the "Siècle des Lumières" with a vivacious and prophetic mind which was to greatly kindle the radiance of this era.

A notable, he revealed himself through intimidating titles, "Président à Mortier [17]" in the Bordeaux parliament, venerated member of the *Académie*. But let us not forget that he was born *extra muros*, in the countryside surrounded by flat lands, at the *La Brède* castle, and that he never ceased to lay claim to his earthly and winegrowing roots: "I like being at La Brède; there, my money seems to be beneath my feet. In Paris, it feels like I carry it on my shoulders."

One could not better assert one's vocation of master-builder, of pioneer. He did not conceive the morrow's society, of which he premeditated the bases in *Esprit des Lois [18]*, as a theorist of some obscure utopia but as a practitioner of the future, with such wisdom, such pragmatism that our modern times still bear witness to the prophetic essence of his prescience.

As if on purpose, not far from *La Brède*, an ideal metropolis started to emerge, under the enlightened guardianship of the first of the "Grands Intendants". Builders as well, stone planters, slowly eradicating the dark medieval cluster. Ausone's Burdigala

resuscitated in a more imposing way yet, with colonnades, palaces, pagan gods, monumental porticos, star shaped avenues… A crossroads boldly opened onto a new world, planetary, "connecting Europe, the US, Asia and Africa".

➡ *Montesquieu and his Castle at La Brède*

By calling "rue Esprit-des-Lois [19]" one of her most noble arteries, Bordeaux accomplished what no other city in the world, perhaps, had thought of yet: to name an architectural ensemble resolutely facing the future after a masterpiece of the mind.

In spite of such splendour, the city slowly crystallized herself in her unaccomplished destiny. The vast design of an ideal metropolis conceived

RUE ESPRIT-DES-LOIS

Previously called rue Porte-Richelieu, this street runs along the Grand Theatre, the old Préfecture and leads to the Place Jean-Jaurès. With the street's current name, the City of Bordeaux pays homage to the works of Montequieu ("l'Esprit des Lois"), and at the same time to one of her greatest writers.

by the last of the "Intendants", Dupré de Saint Maur, was never to be achieved.

Throughout the 19th Century, as if compelled by her own reflection, Bordeaux turned complaisant. Admittedly she continued to fascinate passing-by guests: Stendhal, Hölderlin, Gautier, Hugo especially, whose aquiline gaze crystallized her once and for all in a striking shortcut: "take Versailles, mix it

with Anvers, and you will have Bordeaux".

The *Bordeaux* person took many years to appear, with *éclat*, in one of her own revolted and fascinated sons, the first to dare proclaim "I love and loathe Bordeaux like myself".

The secret face of the city was sensed by François Mauriac very early on, when still a schoolboy he would slip on the sleepy streets' wet pavement of the "aubes navrantes [20]" between the tall soot coloured buildings. Motherly city, "matron" city, the fertile influence of which he would never cease his entire life to both cherish and exorcise.

"Les maisons, les rues de Bordeaux, ce sont les événements de ma vie, Bordeaux, c'est mon enfance et mon adolescence détachées de moi. [21]"

It took some time before "Bordeaux-la-superbe [22]" recognized herself in such a mirror without neither a sense of complaisance nor failing. But today, in one of her Public Garden alleys, the bronze effigy of the eternal rebel chiselled by the hand of Zadkine testifies to their ineffaceable and mutual influence.

And thus, nearly two millennia apart, was restored the direct dialogue, the "hand to heart" sensorial communication as sketched by Ausone the precursor.

Following Mauriac, diverse spokespersons hurtled through this fractal in a wall of respectful silence: Louis Emié, Jean Forton, André Berry, Philippe Jullian, Jean-Paul Michel, Philippe Sollers, Christine de Rivoyre, Paul Leuquet, Jean Lacouture, Pierre Veilletet, Michel Ohl, Philippe Coudray, Bernard Delvaille, Jean-Marie Planes, Michel Rey… all, in their own manner, calling for "Droit de Cité [23]".
From then on, room for doubt is no

more: the "Bordeaux Persona" does indeed exist, built from signs as much as stones, multiple and unique, innumerable and solitary, fiercely creating her own vulnerable soul with the ephemeral heart of the living.

➤ *The Great Bordeaux Library*

THE BIG BELL

Sheltered inside a fortified door built during the 12th Century, it stands as a reminder that Bordeaux was surrounded by ramparts for centuries. Two meters high, nearly two meters in diameter in its lower part and weighing 7800 kg, it was cast in 1775 and remains one of the city's symbolic features.

MADE IN

by.Marie-Laure.Hubert-Nasser

BORDEAUX

Is Bordeaux a brand name? Is it a fine wine, or a beacon? Such could be our query to specialists from the world over, they would undoubtedly answer with more questions yet! Has this city established its own identity, promoted its heritage, allowed its talents to vibrate, or worked on building a powerful image? The question remains as the product is original in a prolix and highly competitive environment. Perhaps one of its most recent achievements hailing from both contemporary and past cultural heritage, namely the water mirror, could offer us a glimpse of what the future holds…

➡ *The* Cours du Chapeau rouge *by night*

*Mirror, mirror on the wall,
when the fine drizzle ceases, will
you unveil your secret? Mirror, oh
my beautiful mirror, pray tell if
Bordeaux "the brand" already
is or will never be?*

*Miroir, oh beau miroir, quand la
fine bruine s'éparpillera, pourrais-
tu le voile lever sur ton secret?
Miroir, oh beau miroir, dis-moi
si Bordeaux "la marque" est déjà
ou ne sera pas?*

Thus one could, under the pretext of
exploring the brand, tell the enchanting
story of a city born within the heart of
an earthly paradise and which, stirring
out of a long long sleep, begun on a
journey that would lead it to its own
stamp, its very emblem. Blessed by the
gods and Dionysus [24] in particular, this
city carried in its genetic code the
necessary elements to make for a
homogeneous and competitive brand.
As far away as people would dwell from,
all as one would repeat the words
"Bordeaux", "châteaux", "beaux [25]".
Sometimes the eulogy would differ
slightly, as visitors attracted by the wine
would depict the city using such lexicon
as "beautiful robe, silken wine, spicy,
mineral, fine, pleasing, velvety,
crimson, amaranthine".

Still others would prefer to the
beverage the wonderful line of the

➡ *The* Galerie bordelaise

eighteenth's century
façades, their proud
sunny stones
magnified in the
silvery river's
troubled water.
Such vitality!

Come to think of
it, this "ke c bô [26]"
universal consensus
did not really
embody all the
creative attributes of
a truly competitive
brand. Were all these
qualifiers tirelessly
uttered by bewitched
visitors really
enough? Could such
a promise of beauty
single Bordeaux out
from a myriad of
other cities in need
of recognition?

A brand is
undoubtedly

THE GRAND THEATRE

The Bordeaux Opera, long called "Grand Theatre", replaced the old theatre which disappeared in a fire in 1755. The Duc de Richelieu, Governor of Guyenne, entrusted in 1773 his architect Victor Louis to build the new City Theatre. A real work-of-art in composition, its conception remains prodigious in stage mechanical equipment as well as in acoustic and visual perspectives. Everything in this theatre indicates how Louis sought to nestle audiences as in a jewel case.

➡ *The Higher Level Court*

constructed by the will of those who create it! Like the designer's artwork, it cannot come to life without a purpose. Had Bordeaux the "desired city" been fashioned by the expert hand of a few marketing geniuses?

Surprisingly for several decades now Bordeaux has been arousing interest among the greatest men in this world. It is common knowledge that certain historical treasures decline in the hands of power as they gradually lose their unique essence. Bordeaux, under the steely grip of a daring gallant (Jacques Chaban Delmas), still enjoys a youthful blush. Driven with mastery by the one who believed in its stamp and character (Alain Juppé), the city leaned on its many talents to soar. Proud of having reconquered its image, Bordeaux envisioned, line after line, every contour of its own emblem.

The quay's façades reclaim, the river's

TIDAL BASINS

The Submarine Base

In the 19th Century, in order to deal with tidal problems, the Bordelaise people planned to build a tidal basin to facilitate ship loading and unloading on constantly level waters, as already existed in the London docks. The first one was inaugurated in 1879, the second in 1911. North of the latter, a submarine base was constructed during the German occupancy.

taming, the sandy stones revival, the light shining again, the tramway design…, all key items of this emergent product from the tourist industry.

And then the miracle happened. Dazzled by its own brilliant glow, the city turned around. Standing tall before lacerating narrow streets, Bordeaux embraced its destiny and contemplated its own reflection in the iridescent shimmer of an eleven thousand square feet granite slab covered with water or steam. Ideal "PoS [27]" for a city with such a striking image, set out to reconquer the world.

But would you believe for one moment that with this "water mirror", the largest in the world, the city had sought the austere translation of a French-style park?

No. Far from being the obsequious mirror of a forlorn beauty, this avant-garde masterpiece reveals a powerful brand, proclaiming to anyone passing by three fundamental values: liberty, creativity and conviviality [28].

41

➡ *The Stone Bridge*

THE STONE BRIDGE

Built under Napoléon 1ˢᵗ and designed by the engineers Deschamps and Billaudel, the Stone Bridge facilitates the crossing of the Garonne river. 486 meters long, with no less than 17 arches (the number of letters in Napoléon Bonaparte), it was first crossed in 1822 and remained the only bridge until the Saint-Jean Bridge was built in 1965.

➡ *The* La Bastide *district*

Colors

from Bordeaux

by · Louise · Gabriel

A Foggy Morning

STROLLING along the stone bridge on a pale foggy morning, gazing at the buildings deploying their façades before you, standing proud and majestic along the Garonne river and her sandy waters tumbling with sparkly and dangerous whirlpools.

Singling out the silhouettes of a few passers-by on the sunken quays, musing upon the city's awakening merely to accompany your solitude, your gaze drifting about the abandoned shores while the river runs into the wide ocean. Observing bright sparkles of light reflected on muddy banks as they pierce through the soft morning fog. Knowing within oneself the tide is low, and blissfully thinking that, here, the world reaches perfect landscape harmony, when the ocean etches its oscillations right into the very heart of the port.

Leaning on the parapet, bending a little to catch a better glimpse of the water rushing around the bridge's pillars. Looking up, discerning the river's

45

contour which nonchalantly curls to rest upon the city itself before disappearing into the white and hesitant atmosphere.

At the end of the bridge, descending onto the quays and strolling along the river. In the mist enfolding the watercourse, feeling the sun's warm caress still. Admiring the architecture of the buildings, such classic regularity that it seems one façade endlessly mirrors itself into the horizon. Like a theatre décor ready for a never-ending show, anticipating the light about to shine on the Garonne river.

Searching for the other shore, not distinguishing it quite but rather guessing the darker tree shapes with entangled foliage. Staring ahead beyond the curve of the water and into the invisible horizon. As the white morning breaks, telling oneself the ocean drank the entire river during the night.

Walking on along the quays passing other pedestrians, anonymous forms with opaque density come to disturb the first rays of light. Remembering that just a little farther the rectilinear perspective of the proud buildings bathing in terracotta elegance includes a semi-circular plaza, at the heart of which stands the "Trois Grâces" fountain. Guessing their attractive figures and distinguishing the soft sizzling of the water as it generously tumbles out of the jugs they carry.

Stopping a while to admire the riverbank: deep fissures running along its muddy, wet and shiny strata, the water merging into the yellow shade of the city's stones.

→ *The left bank quays façades*

Moving on still towards the heart of this maze and making out, lying about the quay, a water mirror covered with steam swirls rising from the ground, floating about the delimited area, prisoners of an invisible line, perhaps even forgotten by the morning fog as it disappears into the sky.

THE TROIS GRÂCES FOUNTAIN

Designed by Visconti and created in 1869, the Trois Grâces Fountain represents "Zeus' daughters" Aglaé, Euphrosyne and Thalie. It is situated on the plaza which was named Place de la Bourse after the revolution.

47.

A large sailboat

The whirls ever so slightly losing their substance, revealing the thin liquid surface, light and transparent in which the rectilinear building façades shine, followed by the plaza and the shapely fountain statues. In such perfect symmetry, discovering the city upside down, resting upon her silver roofs, lengthened by three turrets with willowy peaks darting into the sky.

Walking around the installation and, facing the river, watching among the last vaporous filaments, as if slowly stirring from the mirror, not its shores deserted by the waters nor its warm terracotta shades, nor even the mysterious, distant and quite unreachable shore dissimulated by the trees opposite, but an immense deep and luminous sky accentuated yet by the absence of the slightest identifiable element, a clean sky as can be seen from the open ocean.

In the lain mirror, looking for the river and finding the ocean.

➡ *On the Water Mirror, facing the Place de la Bourse*

➡ *The Aquitaine Bridge*

➡ *Docked cruise ship*

➡ *Left bank quays*

A few adresses

Museums

MUSÉE D'AQUITAINE
20, cours Pasteur
Bordeaux
05 56 01 51 00

MUSÉE DES ARTS DÉCORATIFS
39, rue Bouffard
Bordeaux
05 56 00 72 50

MUSÉE DES BEAUX-ARTS
Jardins de la Mairie
20, cours d'Albret
Bordeaux
05 56 51 71 70

BASE SOUS-MARINE
Boulevard Alfred Daney
Bordeaux
05 56 11 11 50

CAPC MUSÉE D'ART CONTEMPORAIN
7, rue Ferrère
Bordeaux
05 56 00 81 50

MUSÉE DU VIN ET DU NÉGOCE
41, rue Borie
Bordeaux
05 56 90 19 13

MUSÉE NATIONAL DES DOUANES
1, place de la Bourse
Bordeaux
05 56 48 82 82

MUSÉUM D'HISTOIRE NATURELLE
Closed from the end of June 2009
until 2012 due to renovation
Hôtel de Lisleferme
5, place Bardineau
Bordeaux
05 56 48 26 37

➠ *Restaurants*

LE PAVILLON DES BOULEVARDS
120, rue Croix de Seguey
Bordeaux
05 56 81 51 02

LE CHAPON FIN
5, rue Montesquieu
Bordeaux
05 56 79 10 10

GRAVELIER
114, cours de Verdun
Bordeaux
05 56 48 17 15

AU BONHEUR DU PALAIS
74, rue Paul-Louis Lande
Bordeaux
05 56 94 38 63

UP AND DOWN
25, rue Pas Saint-Georges
Bordeaux
05 56 52 87 48

L'AUBERG'INN
245, rue Turenne
Bordeaux
05 56 81 97 86

RAGAZZI
9, quai Richelieu
Bordeaux
05 56 30 25 25

LE GRAND THÉATRE
29, rue Esprit des Lois
Bordeaux
05 56 81 30 30

LA GRAND'VIGNE
Les Sources de Caudalie
Martillac
05 57 83 83 83

LE BISTROY
3, place Camille Hostein
Bouliac
05 57 97 06 06

L'ESTACADE
Quai de Queyries
Bordeaux
05 57 54 02 50

LA CONCORDE
50, rue du Maréchal Joffre
Bordeaux
05 56 44 68 97

LE CAFÉ DU MUSÉE CAPC
7 rue Ferrière
Bordeaux
05 56 44 71 61

MOSHI MOSHI
8, place Fernand Lafargue
Bordeaux
05 56 79 22 91

BISTROT D'ELOI
1, rue Esprit des lois
Bordeaux
05 56 52 45 34

BRASSERIE L'EUROPE
THE REGENT GRAND HÔTEL
Place de la comédie
Bordeaux
05 57 30 43 47

JEAN-MARIE AMAT
Château du Prince Noir
26, rue Raymond Lis
Lormont
05 56 06 12 52

LE SAINT JAMES
3, place Camille Hostein
Bouliac
05 57 97 06 00

➠ *Michel Portos, Head of Kitchen at the Saint James*

LE CAFÉ DU THÉATRE
3, place Pierre Renaudel
Square Jean Vauthier
Bordeaux
05 57 95 77 20

LE CLOS D'AUGUSTA
339, rue Georges Bonnac
Bordeaux
05 56 96 32 51

LA TUPINA
6-8, rue Porte de la Monnaie
Bordeaux
05 56 91 56 37

➠ Gourmet Shopping

LE CAFÉ MARITIME
1 quai Armand Lalande
Bassin à flot n°1
Bordeaux
05 57 10 20 40

LE SALADIN
16bis, rue Latour
Bordeaux
05 56 52 87 21

LE CAFÉ GOURMAND
3, rue Buffon
Bordeaux
05 56 79 23 85

AU SARMENT
50, rue Lande
Saint-Gervais
05 57 43 44 73

CORDEILLAN BAGES
Route des Châteaux
Pauillac
05 56 59 24 24

L'HOSTELLERIE DE PLAISANCE
Place du Clocher
Saint-Emilion
05 57 55 07 55

LA CAPE
9, allée de la Morlette
Cenon
05 57 80 24 25

ANTOINE
19, cours Portal
Bordeaux
05 56 81 43 19
Pâtisserie

COUSIN
88, Bd Georges Pompidou
Bordeaux
05 56 98 67 64
Pâtisserie

BAILLARDRAN
29, rue Porte Dijeaux
Bordeaux
05 56 52 87 45
Pâtisserie

CADIOT-BADIE
26, allée de Tourny
Bordeaux
05 56 44 24 22
Chocolate

CHOCOLATERIE SAUNION
56, cours Georges Clémenceau
Bordeaux
05 56 48 05 75
Chocolate

BOUTIQUE PIERRE OTEIZA
77, rue Condillac
Bordeaux
05 56 52 38 76
Basque Delicacies

BADIE
62, allées de Tourny
Bordeaux
05 56 52 23 72
Wines

L'INTENDANT
2, allées de Tourny
Bordeaux
05 56 48 01 29
Wines

BORDEAUX MAGNUM
3, rue Gobineau
Bordeaux
05 56 48 00 06
Wines

BERNARD MAGREZ
216, av. du Dr Nancel Pénard
Pessac
05 57 26 43 04
Wines

BLACK SEA CAVIAR
5, rue Martignac
Bordeaux
05 56 51 20 56
Caviar

JEAN D'ALOS
4, rue Montesquieu
Bordeaux
05 56 44 29 66
Cheese

⇒ Brunch

⇒ Art Galleries

⇒ Hotels

LE PETIT COMMERCE
22, rue du Parlement Saint-Pierre
Bordeaux
05 56 79 76 58

LE BAR À VIN
3, cours du 30 juillet
Bordeaux
05 56 00 43 47

L'AUTRE SALON DE THÉ
11 rue des Remparts
Bordeaux
05 56 48 55 43

CAMBRIDGE ARMS
27, rue Rode
Bordeaux
05 56 51 19 22

L'ORANGERIE
Cours de Verdun, Jardin Public
Bordeaux
05 56 48 24 41

PAIN&CIE
64, rue des Remparts
Bordeaux
09 64 37 78 77

ARRÊT SUR L'IMAGE
Quai Armand Lalande
Bordeaux
05 56 69 16 48

CORTEX ATHLETICO
20, rue Ferrère
Bordeaux
05 56 94 31 89

LA GALERIE ROUGE
19, rue du Professeur Demons
Bordeaux
06 87 46 02 29

LE TROISIÈME OEIL
17, rue des Remparts
Bordeaux
05 56 44 32 23

SEEKO'O
54, quai de Bacalan
Bordeaux
05 56 39 07 07

THE REGENT GRAND HOTEL
2, place Comédie
Bordeaux
05 57 30 44 44

SOFITEL AQUITANIA
1, avenue Jean-Gabriel Domergue
Bordeaux Lac
05 56 69 66 66

LA MAISON BORD'EAUX
113, rue Albert-Barraud
Bordeaux
05 56 44 00 45
Guest house

LE SAINT JAMES
3, place Camille Hostein
Bouliac
05 57 97 06 00

Antique Dealer in the Saint-Michel district

Market in the Saint-Michel district

➡ *The famous "Sainte-Catherine" street*

➤ *The* Place de la Boutse *square on a warm summer evening*

➡ *Bordeaux as seen from the Pey-Berland Tower*

Fenwick House

Ah, you English you've always been here !

by. Kevin. Desmond

The **Frog & Rosbif**

HONI SOIT QUI PEU Y BOIT

WELL, ALMOST ALWAYS.

It all began about 850 years ago, in 1152, when Aliénor or Eleanor, the Duchess of Aquitaine married the French-speaking Count Henri Plantagenet just before he became King Henry II of England. This made Bordeaux an English possession which it would remain for three centuries.

During this time, the city flourished. Impressive fleets of English-built ships transported wine and weapons to English ports like London, Exeter, Bristol, Dartmouth, Hull and Chester. They would return with wool, dried fish, Cornish tin and lead to Bordeaux. Sometimes, when the wine barrels which had acted as ship's ballast were discharged, the replacement ballast, good quality English quarry stone, was taken back and purchased by Bordeaux builders for constructions inside the walled city.

In 1160, Richard Plantagenet, Eleanor's son, nicknamed "The Lionheart", took up residence in the Ombrière Palace, residence of the Dukes of Gascony, surrounding himself with clergy, aristocracy and English Mayors of

Bordeaux, such as Pierre Bukton, Thomas of Sandwich, Thomas Swynburne, and Henry Redford.

So Bordeaux became the capital of an independent sovereign state under Edward, Prince of Wales, whose dark armoury earned him the name "The Black Prince".

Edward had been born in Woodstock, and his son Richard of Bordeaux later ruled as King Richard II of England.

Following a long drawn-out war of one hundred years, in 1452 the English lost the Battle of Castillon and Bordeaux became French.

Bordeaux began to regain its popularity in 18th Century England, once again through its wine, known in London as the "New French Claret". Indeed in England, the words claret and Bordeaux became synonymous.

Among those who profited from this new trade were several English-speaking entrepreneurs who set up in Bordeaux. In 1717 from Scotland came William Johnston, aged 17, who set a wine-dealing business carried on by his descendants, most of whom were called Nathaniel.

In 1725 came Thomas Barton, then Abraham Lawton, both from Ireland. And so the "wine geese" flew in – Brown, Mitchell, O'Lanyer etc. Indeed by the late 1700's we find 20 Irishmen and 20 Irishwomen and only 2 Englishman – residing and working in the Chartrons area of the city.

In 1732, Freemasonry arrived in the city. Captain Martin Kelly, Nicholas Stainton and Jonathan Robinson called their Lodge, "L'Anglaise". Eleven years later it had been changed to "La Française".

Indeed in 1763 a French playwright, Charles-Simon Favart wrote a satirical comedy called *"L'Anglais à Bordeaux"* where the actor who portrayed Mr Summers had to speak French with an English accent to the raucous laughter of the Comédie Française audience.

Sensible to trends, Messrs Stevens and Jacob had opened the "Hôtel

→ *The* Prince Noir *Castle, home to Jean-Marie Amat's restaurant*

d'Angleterre" at N°10 Cours Tourny in central Bordeaux. Among their many English-speaking visitors on tour around Europe, a certain Mrs Cradock in 1785. During the French Revolution, this establishment discreetly changed its name to the "Hôtel Franklin!" after Benjamin Franklin, then US Commissar in France. In 1791 the Hotel was visited by Prince Frederick-Auguste, son of His Majesty the King George of England, travelling under the assumed name of the Count de Dielphos.

Not far away, in 1797, Dutchman David-Christophe Meyer had built a fine house whose name he changed

from the "*Café of one Thousand Columns*" to the "*Café Anglais*" where of course English was spoken.

In 1829, the Anglo-Irish residents living near the Pavé des Chartrons, began to hold Anglican services in a converted barn, provided by the Johnston family. By 1841 several parishioners had financed the building of St. Nicholas Church in the Course Xavier Arnozan where Sunday services would be held for the next 148 years.

The tradition of English-speaking Sunday worship continues even today with the Chaplaincy of the Aquitaine.

Also during the 1830's parishioner David Johnston, also Mayor of

➡ *The Submarine Base*

Bordeaux, financed a pottery works at the Moulin des Chartrons. Ships which had transported wine to England, then returned with the raw materials and some of the patterns and motifs on the china porcelain were very English, even if the 700-strong workforce was local. For example, tea pots and milk jugs with scenes of horse-racing and fox-hunting. Somehow the idea did not catch on and Johnston sold the failing enterprise to his technical manager Jules Vieillard.

Also frequently in evidence English-style furniture such as secretaries and bureau-cabinets in British Honduras mahogany, clocks with claw-style legs and wallpaper designs…With wealth came leisure. From 1845, Messrs Guestier and Fould directed the Société d'Encouragement du "Club" Bordelais, beginning with horse-racing for cups presented by the Johnstons around the Le Bouscat Racecourse. The "Steeple-chases" Society and the "Trotting" Club would follow.

Elsewhere in July 1852, Johnston with his yacht *La Fée-aux-Roses* and Mr Cutter with the *Amazone* enjoyed the first regatta to be seen off Arcachon.

65

In 1863, inspired by the Oxford versus Cambridge Varsity Boat Race, the Burdigala "Rowing Club" established its "Boat House" on Bordeaux's quai Paludate. Here le "cox could train eight oarsmen or sculls".

To get around the town, you could board a horse-drawn tramway, one of 120 such vehicles, owned and managed by the English "Tramways & General Works Company Ltd."

On the cultural side, an Irish-born priest, the Abbé Patrick-John O'Reilly, exhausted himself researching and writing *"A Complete History of Bordeaux"* in 6 volumes, published two years' after his early death.

In 1890, wine courtiers, Guestier and Lawton, had two houses built, side-by-side in Floirac on the other side of the River. Guestier had a nine-hole golf course landscaped into his grounds, while Edouard Lawton created a lawn tennis court: the first time that Wimbledon style lawn tennis was ever played in France.

In 1897, Lawton created a second tennis court in Cauderan, suburb of Bordeaux. Its "Villa Primrose" was run like an English country club, its presidency handed down through the Lawton dynasty. It would later organise field hockey. Three years later, again in Cauderan, Messrs Palmer-Sambourne, White, Bryce and Martin had the lande

➡ *The* Primrose *House*

de Pezau landscaped into what they called le "Golf Club" de Bordeaux. Terminology was and ever since has included phrases like "taking a n° 4 iron to hit the ball onto the green." In case you are thinking all this was only for the elite, we should not leave

out the "Football Club Bordelaise".

To get to these events, you could board an electric tramway driven not by un conducteur but by a "wattman"!

By this time, one William Calendreau Walton, originally from Macclesfield, England, had built up a business in Bordeaux Bastide assembling and supplying agricultural machinery. With the arrival of the automobile, Walton was one of the first to be seen motoring around the city in a car built at his works. He was one of the Founder members of the Automobile Club of Bordeaux and became its Treasurer in 1900.

Ironically, during the 20th Century, there were very few English-speaking folk in Bordeaux, 133 in all, and these were split in half – wealthy wine dealers or the servant class. Indeed no important French Bordeaux family, calling their eldest sons "James", speaking English as a first language, would be seen without an English nanny, butler and/or cocher/chauffeur. Philippe Jullian who grew up in Bordeaux at the time would later satirise this "anglomanie" in his book "*My Lord*" dealing with an eccentric dandy Lord Tanquerville!

When the Nazi Germans entered Bordeaux in June 1940, the English had fled the city and the occupying Reich might have thought not a single "Englander" threatened them. They were wrong. In December 1942, two camouflaged kayaks, crewed by courageous English commandoes secretly crept into Bordeaux harbour and used limpet mines to sabotage five German merchant ships that had broken the Royal navy blockade on France. A memorial to those "Cockleshell Heroes" can be found on the quays.

Not long after the Armistice, in July 1947, a small group of 2 teachers and 27 pupils set out from Fairfield Grammar School, Bristol – destination Bordeaux. Two months later, Bordeaux pupils had gone over to Bristol. It was a twinning and exchange system which has since led to thousands of students learning French or English.

Among the pop songs which emerged from the 1960's, we should not leave out the 45 rpm single "Anglomanie" sung by A Frenchman calling himself "Richard de Bordeaux"! (not to be confused with today's American singer Richard Bordeaux of Los Angeles)

In 1977 the city's Galerie des Beaux-Arts put on a very popular exhibition "La Peinture Britannique: Gainsborough to Bacon."

As for today, in the 21st Century, Bordeaux holds onto its English trends. Its new law courts, "Tribunal de Grande Instance" were designed by a British architect, Richard Rogers.
And then there are the pubs…

And all the way through this, the sounds of that delightful accent which opens the imposing doors to those who proudly and fondly recall their descent from the distant days when Bordeaux was an English colony!

➡ *The decorative Arts Museum (1779)*

➡ *The* Fort du Hâ *tower (15th century)*

➡ *The Higher Level Court*

Contemporary Art

by · Marie - Laure · Hubert - Nasser

Inspiration. Imagination. Contemporary art in Bordeaux starts with a place. Central. Mythical. The CAPC (Contemporary Arts Museum of Bordeaux). Clear archways bear past scribbles still. Colonial goods warehouse in former times, today a nest for creativity to come. Rustling. Whispering. Contemplating. True happiness stolen from passing time. A flight of stairs preceding a magnificent shaded patio and refined restaurant, revisited by Andrée Putman. Sheer delight.

Surprise. Fun with art. With an object. Large. Powerful. A sculpture at the crossroads between contemporary art and comic books. Xavier Veilhan's Blue Lion. Emblematic. Dreamlike. Oversized. Sitting enthroned upon a fast changing area. A picture must be taken between his giant paws!

Boldly strange. Looming illusion in a quiet landscape. "La maison aux personnages ^{29}" by Ilya Kabakov. Snooping. Gazing through the window, leading the lives of imaginary characters. Desire, discover, acquire. Two must-be-seen locations. "Freeze frame". Art gallery where collages, engraving, sculptures and photography interchange with one another. In a renovated storehouse. Huge. Odd. Breathtaking river view. And then the "Cortex Athletico". Young works, bright future. An emergent gallery hosting tomorrow's Greats.

CAPC
THE

In 1973, Jacques Chaban-Delmas, then Mayor of Bordeaux, supported the project of a young art-gallery owner, Jean-Louis Froment, who ambitioned to create an Arts Centre for temporary experimental exhibitions. Located in an exceptional architectural décor, this welcoming place for artists aimed at widening the specificities of contemporary artistic forms to large audiences. The Centre accommodated all forms of modern creation such as dance, theatre, music and even fashion. In 1984, the CAPC was granted the status of Museum, which confirmed the success of its politics and international fame.

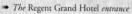
The Regent Grand Hotel *entrance*

Located just opposite the Opéra National de Bordeaux (the Grand Théâtre) The Regent Grand Hotel Bordeaux is reclaiming its place as the most majestic hotel in the city. The hotel has undergone a comprehensive and faithful restoration which respects its colourful history while offering a level of luxury and elegance never before experienced.

The Regent Grand Hotel

arch i

by . B o u b a c a r . S e c k

➡ *The left bank quays façades*

tecture

ARCHITECTURE is the great book of humanity, as Victor Hugo used to say. These words, by the author of "Les Misérables", are particularly suited to the city of Bordeaux. There, you can admire Montesquieu's Suppliques [30] engraved in stone, on his wish to see *les hommes se guérir de leurs préjugés* [31]. Thus we discover the great library's canopies change into calligraphic essays by Montaigne.

By indulging in the generative grammar of the legs, a sentence that strollers by and tourists can read in the city's open book, one discovers a particularly well-preserved city. Few pages were torn apart during bombings and dramatic events in the past centuries. This contributes to the City of Lights' pride in owning one of the most beautiful and coherent architectural and cultural ensembles in France.

City of Lights indeed. But the lights are not those emanating from eye-catching neons. Rather they stem from stones, those which transform medieval grim and dark streets, melancholic alleys and desperate dead-ends. They shine from the golden moon lain on the port, magnifying the stony bridge. They glow from the stones as they illuminate 18th Century ironworks, revealing façades which such rich features that one can read economic developments and social complexities in them.

Early morns, the city darkened by gray rains. Cobblestones brushed by the secular passing of men shine silvery gleams. Consoles in the shape of ready to pounce wild animals, slaves' effigies or again Bacchus mascarons hooked on the classic façades can play Narcissus with this infinite water mirror. This moiré empire, once dried up by the return of warm and full of promise sunny days, gives way to another mirror drawn by an inspired landscaper: showstopper evoking both a Spanish *paseo* and a *Promenade des Anglais* on quays rediscovered after a long slumber. The city assumes both stories from north and south.

One can also enjoy a great view from watchtowers, phantom castles and the "Cité Mondiale" terrace. There Bordeaux, usually secretive and discreet, displays her intimacy. Church steeples

➡ *The* Place des Quinconces

pricked up like urban ears unwind their rosaries. Sunlounges thirsting for light, slated and yellowish brown tin roofs, speckled or brushed tiles, private life nestled on rooftops, brick chimneys restless in their solitude unveil their secrets before our curious eyes. Bordeaux echoes at our feet as salsa bars, pubs and bodegas refute the tenacious belief she is a city huddled upon herself.

In the distance, one can see the vine-woven earth on which the iconoclast Jean Nouvel raised the Bouliac Hotel, reminiscence from neighboring tobacco barns. A little closer, the Garonne River

➡ *On Parliament Square*

➡ *The Saint James Hotel in Bouliac, built by Jean Nouvel*

tenderly welcomes the illustrious ships Cuauhtémoc, Belém and summer saturnalia fairs. On its other bank, promenades, botanic gardens and greenhouses where plants burgeon offer lanceolate rosebuds. There, the entire architecture breathes a green hand.

And when the natural curve from the river meets the *Sustainable Development Arch*, the city emerges from past centuries' nostalgia to enter a new era of "reality utopia". Bordeaux unfolds her architectural history and innovative projects before her guests.

Today the show is not only nestled within Gabriel's perfectly proportioned *Place de la Bourse*, but it also happens on the steps of the Grand Italian Theatre by Victor Louis, and the port banks. After having generously welcomed the Art Nouveau style and the post-

79

➡ *The Rohan Palace. Former French Prime Minister Alain Juppé is Mayor of Bordeaux since 1995.*

modernism from the fifties, the city prudently entered into a resolutely contemporary phase. The *Cité de la Justice* by Sir Richard Rogers announced a time of change: built upon the *Fort du Hâ* ruins, the city like an alchemist combines stone, metal, wood and copper in perfect harmony with the Cathedral and the *Palais Rohan,* siege of the city's First Magistrate. Her seven domes where society expiates faults are offered to the city, open without ever being indecent.

The stage directing continues today with the Seeko Hotel. The streamlined Corian igloo, frosty and frozen as if drowned in blizzard, dances from neoclassic respect to irreverence with dazzling whiteness. This virginal color streams right onto the quays, illuminating the city. Between these two fundamental acts, a thousand original architectures are to be discovered behind the old wooden doors: the *Annonciade Convent* praises the renovated conventual architecture, the *ZAC des Chartrons* demonstrates urban transformation and renewal qualities, lofts reinvent our way of living, shadowed cellars become taverns, stalls and *bourgeois* houses surprise us…

The new rearranged plazas and the wide restructured arteries prove that a streetcar named "desire of humanity" can move the city. This strange blue and black domesticated snake helps crossing Bordeaux agglomeration faster. It mainly connects areas which link with the hyper centre was formerly weak.

→ *Part of the Higher Level Court designed by the architect Richard Rogers*

➡ *The Seeko'o Hotel, on the quays, designed by the architectural practice King Kong*

Bordeaux is a great book of souvenirs, the authors of which tactfully left some pages blank. The city fills our eyes with loving, charming faces, with unforgettable landscapes, with sunset imprints and raw emotion, to unite, as François Mauriac used to say, "everything one needs to write", everything one needs to live.

➡ *The* Place de la Victoire *square*

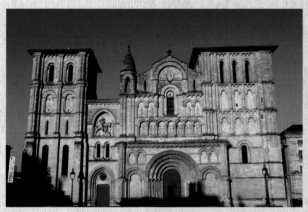

➡ *The Sainte-Croix church, located in the Sainte-Croix district*

➡ *Part of the left bank quays*

THE BOTANICAL GARDEN

Landscape Architect Catherine Mosbach and Architect Françoise-Hélène Jourda designed this innovative garden, a far cry from traditional botanical gardens: laid out in several distinct areas, it offers a journey into Ecology, Sustainable Development and Knowledge. It is located on the right bank of Bordeaux.

tecture

SAINT-ANDRÉ CATHEDRAL

It was built between the 6th and the 13th Centuries. It seems this site hosted several cathedrals since the first bishop in the 4th Century. It is in this particular one, on July 25th 1137, that Alienor wedded Louis le Jeune, who himself was to become Louis the Seventh.

As the basement was quite unsteady, the vaults had to be reconstructed thus giving the walls much buttress support. Imposing, it remains in the line of the Latin Cross Plan.

Painters

by.Louise.Gabriel

In the city ...

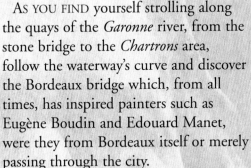

AS YOU FIND yourself strolling along the quays of the *Garonne* river, from the stone bridge to the *Chartrons* area, follow the waterway's curve and discover the Bordeaux bridge which, from all times, has inspired painters such as Eugène Boudin and Edouard Manet, were they from Bordeaux itself or merely passing through the city.

At the beginning of the 19th Century, Pierre Lacour (1745-1814), key member of the Bordelaise life (he founded the Free Drawing school, also Conservator of the Painting Museum), represented the majestic façade of the buildings on the *Chartrons* quay. From looking at his painting called "*Vue du quai des Chartrons* [32]" (1804-1806 / Bordeaux Fine Arts Museum), one understands that Bordeaux was a large merchants port in which many three-masted, corvettes or schooners would stop. The quays were full of life and would offer passersby the continuous spectacle of people from diverse trades going about their business by the riverside, around multiple embarkations, hailing from far away countries or en route to exotic destinations.

At the end of the 19th Century, the Bordeaux quays were repeatedly painted by Alfred Smith (1854-1936), Bordelaise artist originated from Great Britain who managed to transcribe various impressions of the *Garonne* shores beyond realistic precision, at different times of the day, evoking paintings by William Turner. For example, in his painting called "*Tramway devant les Quinconces par temps de pluie* [33]" (1890 / Collection Particulière), in a damp-saturated atmosphere, one can make out the Saint-Michel church's

→ *Bordeaux City quays*

arrow at the back, the mats of the accosted ships and the cranes, indicating the port's commercial activity. A whiff of modernity is brought by the tramway sailing on the wet road and the hurried or solitary passersby quickening their step along the two prows, erected like proud lighthouses facing the river.

In the 20th Century, the port was also painted by Albert Marquet (1875-1947). Born in Bordeaux, friend of Matisse, this artist could be compared to Cézanne in his manner of portraying things not merely as his eye saw them but rather as he himself felt them, as he lived them. He was considered to be the most classical of the *Fauve* painters, who could materialize reality with a free and impulsive use of colour. But on his painting called *"Le port de Bordeaux vu du quai des Queyries* [34] *"* (1924 / Bordeaux Fine Arts Museum), he opted for soft, silvery and sandy shades to convey a liquid harmony impression between sky and river.

At the same time, André Lhote (1885-1962), Bordelaise painter from cubist inspiration, realized several repre-sentations of the Bordeaux port,

➡ *The tramway and the* Place des Quinconces *Square then and now…*

searching for a balance in the construction of space. On can indeed note this in *"Le port de Bordeaux* [35]*"* (1912 / Collection Particulière) or in other paintings showing a very particular vision of volumes, playing on lines and geometric forms. Besides, in 1956 he created a great fresco called "La Gloire de Bordeaux [36]" which represents the city's dual aspect, both classical and modern. Closely linking creation and reflection in his pictorial research and being a great mediator in his Montparnasse school, he held great influence on Edmond Boissonnet (1906-1995), Bordeaux-born artist among the independent painters who had distanced themselves from the bordelaise academism and who exhibited in the sixties at the renowned *Galerie du Fleuve.* André Lhote also had a certain impact on Tamara Lempicka who took his course in Paris and went on to become a famous post-cubism and *Art-Déco* artist herself.

You can continue walking towards the *Place de la Comédie.* If you turn into the *Allées de Tourny,* take a look at the Bordeaux Grand Theatre: you will enjoy the same angle of view as the one Joseph Basire chose during the 18th Century: in his aquarelle drawing called *"Le Grand Théâtre et le début des Allées Tourny* [37]*"* (1798 / Bordeaux Fine Arts Museum), the antique workmanship of the façade is emphasized by its column portico supporting the statues of the nine Muses and the three goddesses: Juno, Minerva and Venus.

➡ *Joseph Basire's Grand Theatre*

Turning into the small *rue Mautrec*, facing the theatre, you will arrive on the *Place du Chapelet* where you can admire the imposing statue of Francisco de Goya (1746-1828) the famous Spanish painter who took refuge in Bordeaux, having fled the Spanish troubles and the Inquisition. It is in the *Notre-Dame* Church on this same plaza that the Spanish community offered him magnificent funerals.

Then continue to the *Cours de l'Intendance*: at number 51, you will find la casa de Goya. Above the door of his last home, his sculpted face and his dark eyes will stare down at you. In spite of age and intense sufferings, the tormented artist continued to create, among other works, the "*Taureaux de Bordeaux* [38]", beautifully crafted lithography (1825 / Bordeaux Fine Arts Museum). He went on painting and drawing the tragic and whimsical human condition ("*La laitière de Bordeaux* [39]" 1825-1827 / Prado Museum - Madrid). He found inspiration among folks fleetingly met throughout Bordelaise streets and fairs, true living performances on the quays and on the *Place Royale* (nowadays called *Place de la Bourse*).

Francisco de Goya was buried in the great Bordeaux cemetery *La Chartreuse*. In 1880, when the Spanish authorities claimed his body, his tomb was opened revealing a missing head. Among the many hypotheses then evoked to explain such a disappearance, it was supposed that it had been stolen by a spanish artist, who had in 1848 painted a piece called "Craneo de Goya pintado por Fierros", found in an antiques

94

shop. Francisco de Goya's body was repatriated to Spain without its head… Today, the aura of mystery surrounding the artist who was fascinated by human madness and despair remains.

At the end of the *Cours de l'Intendance*, if you cross the *Place Gambetta* and walk to the Saint-Seurin Church, you will find at the end of the street Albert-Barraud the ruins of the *Palais Gallien* [40], formerly called "*Palais de Gallienne*", perhaps a palace in the Antiquity, more probably a roman circus, in any case a badly frequented area until the 18th Century and which the painter Joseph Basire magnificently represented in his painting "*Vue du Palais Gallien* [41]" (1796 / Bordeaux Fine Arts Museum) where realism and imagination intertwine to create an ideal and harmonious vision of the antique ruin.

But from the *Palais Gallien*, you might feel like going to the *Jardin Public* [42] and stroll along its alleys, one of which will take you to the statue of Rosa Bonheur (1822-1899), woman painter born in Bordeaux who represented animals with

➡ Statue of painter Rosa Bonheur.

95

energy and passion, bulls, horses, sheep; she even went to slaughterhouses to paint from model. Free and fiercely attached to her art, she was, during her own lifetime, welcome and honoured in the Parisian painting salons, admired by the most powerful and internationally renowned, notably thanks to one of her paintings "*Le Marché aux chevaux* [43]" which was bought in 1853 by Gambart, then director of the London Gallery. This furthered her fame to the United States.

Looking at the statue representing her seated yet in movement, you will read on her face an expression of both resolve and softness. You will notice her ample skirt and man's jacket, conferring her both a feminine and fiercely independent style.

You can then continue your visit to the Bordeaux Fine Arts Museum, the Aquitaine Museum or the Ornamental Arts Museum, where you will find original masterpieces from some of the painters who accompanied your journey throughout the city.

A walk along the right side of the Garonne River will lead you, some twenty miles farther, to the *Malromé Castle*, where the painter Henri de Toulouse-Lautrec (1864 -1901) would retire in the summertime near his mother, far from his busy Parisian life in the Montmartre cabarets where he would spend long hours sketching and painting beggars, dancers and prostitutes. He was like the Goya of the *Filles de joie* [44]. He even chose the words from the Spanish master "*J'ai vu ça* [45]" as an epigraph for a lithography collection.

96

THE AQUITAINE MUSEUM

Open to the public since 1987, both a History and Ethnography Museum, it hosts varied collections ranging from the Prehistoric and Gallo-Roman periods, through the Dark Ages and into our Modern Times.
There, one can also find numerous Extra-European Civilizations works from Bordeaux' colonial and maritime past.

→ "Salon in the rue des Moulins" (1894)

You can also discover the *Médoc*, north of Bordeaux, narrow strip of land between the ocean and the Gironde estuary. In this region near *Listrac* the bordelaise painter Odilon Redon (1840-1916) spent unforgettable moments during his childhood and youth at the *Domaine de Peyrelebade* [46], family countryside residence. The desolated landscape and the vast solitude from these wild *landes,* lost under too wide a sky, deeply influenced his exacerbated sensitivity, turned towards dream-worlds and contemplation ("*Les barques* [47]", Bordeaux Fine Arts Museum). In this isolated *Médoc* he created these famous drawings called "Noirs [48]", resolutely using charcoal, finding colour too easily attractive. These works depict a surreal world, often phantasmagorical, made of strange and inconceivable apparitions. He later turned his research to colour shades and went on painting a luminous nature with sparkling chimerical flowers, ever seeking the supernatural in every natural thing.

➡ *"Noirs" by Odilon Redon*

➡ *"Les barques" by Odilon Redon*

➡ *Odilon Redon*

➡ *"La laitière de Bordeaux" by Goya*

The "Cours de l'Intendance"

Parliament Square

Thierry

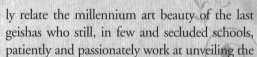

INDEED, HE IS NOT ALONE anymore! But he remains the one who revisited the simple but secular expression: "to dine out", as he undoubtedly invented and implanted a new art of dining. Out from the mysterious cosmos of today's starred chefs, he turned cuisine into a surprising melting pot of flavours and science, intertwining two opposite notions which became twin sisters. Having travelled the world in search of secrets that we will never crack, a lover of the Bordelaise region as much as Japan, he came back with in his steely blue and so generously spirited eyes miracles sprung out of nowhere, and which he now serves in our plates. He knows how to arouse in us, without us even knowing how, this part of our own childhood with tastebud delights from the hands of our great grandmother. Perhaps because he built himself with the heady memory of steamy coffee and warm bread enjoyed with his mother, and also of his grandmother's cooking which he would tastefully and methodically arrange. His cuisine, just like himself, is just a little more complex, a tiny bit more "magical" still. This man turns out to be a rather debonair paradox! He is as much at home in his *médocaine* [49] kitchen sheltered and safeguarded within the domain of Jean-Michel Cazes, with unconditional and doubtless faith since always, as in the middle of Japan with his Master Cutlers, craftsmen of extraordinary sabres which he portrays with tremors in his voice. Perhaps this is so because these two extremes, Bordeaux and Japan alike, once again unite in one and the same essence which seems to spontaneously create, via the eyes, the brain and the hands of Thierry Marx an inexplicable yet fertile and generous alliance. He also knows how to lovingly relate the millennium art beauty of the last geishas who still, in few and secluded schools, patiently and passionately work at unveiling the ultimate secrets of such a special art form with the same meticulousness and acute precision he puts in the realization of his dishes. Work and recognition thus become, associated with a unique character, an art form in itself, and this time, a personal one. And you will notice that the word "dish" will sound dissonant to your ear once you actually taste it! One can only reach the level of creativity and invention one allows oneself, and Thierry knows no limit! As the last mouthful from such an enchanting meal, as if right out of Cocteau's "Beauty and the Beast", disappears, you will intimately know that the next time you renew the experience you will be enchanted by many other discoveries, many other inventions still. This is Thierry Marx' true identity, rooted within the deepest of pasts,

➡ *Thierry Marx, Head of Kitchen at the Cordeillan-Bages restaurant*

keeper of all alchemies. His story his unusual to say the least: after training in Pâtisserie in Paris, he became a *Compagnon du Devoir* [50] in Tours, a soldier in Lebanon, even *convoyeur de fonds* [51]. He then went on to take the *CAP* and *BEP* exams [52] as a *candidat libre*, [53] before forcing the door of the greatest of the French Chefs. He remains an intermittent traveller, always, even while deeply connected to true Bordelaise cuisine. With such profuse journeying he sought to become the one who, starting from the original indelible matter – be it *boeuf carotte, agneau de Pauillac, saucisson médocain* or plain *bouillon de poule* [54] – would transcend and magnify reminiscent tastes into something radically new. You thought you knew the flavour of *ris de veau* [55] as your great grandmother used to cook them in cream with plenty of mushrooms and would serve them with mash topped with a few juicy

cèpes! Well now you find them well sheltered inside a wheat spaghetti corolla, and the *cèpes* combined with truffles have turned into an evanescent liquid sauce. A tiny exotic ingredient unveils new secrets about *ris de veau* that no one, besides himself, ever thought of proposing to your taste buds. And if Chefs mostly remain of the masculine gender, it well may be because they master the warrior art of cooking better than women. And in this discipline too, Thierry will surprise you! By the time lunch or dinner is over, you will have discovered a whole new art of cooking, or at least caught a tantalising glimpse of it. And if you are as lucky as Thierry is cutting-edge, you might just have the pleasure of shaking the master's hand as he, with his warm and lively piercing blue eyes, tells you something you did not know yet about cuisine or even about yourself…

→ *Snails…*

GASTRONOMY

by . Stéphanie . Baudry

Dining in Bordeaux

WHEN SPEAKING of the "Bordelaise Gastronomy", one should not forget the *lamproie* (sea lamprey), the *marchande de vin* entrecôte steak (rib steak in wine sauce), the *pibales* (baby eels) fresh from the Garonne river, and the *cannelés* (a rich crusty caramel dessert)... but of course, the gastronomy of a region cannot be limited to a few dishes only, no matter how delicious and extraordinary as is the case in Bordeaux. It is, first and foremost, a local art form, mastered better than anywhere else, a manner of showing that a city's unique culinary civilization arises out of her own past.

A lover of the Cahors Truffle, Pierre-Jean Pébeyre modestly says: "we do not supply luxury to our Chefs or clientèle, rather we provide raw material." Haute Cuisine is exactly that: transforming and magnifying a raw material into something delightful and original. Classic Bordelaise Cuisine is much more than a few typical local recipes collated in a nice notebook. It includes names, men, women and, last but not least, not-to-be-missed places you are about to discover in these pages.

The "Chapon Fin", located at the heart of the Gold Triangle of Bordeaux on the *Place des Grands Hommes,* is a mythical Bordelaise restaurant which used to be patroned by Toulouse-Lautrec, Sacha Guitry and Sarah Bernhardt. It changed hands a few years ago and is now run by wine expert Jean-Michel Cazes. The decor has been modernized, mixing Bordelaise stone with a refined and surreal ambiance to create an intimate and old-fashioned feel, like Bordeaux had not known for a long time. Nicolas Frion was Thierry Marx' second man for five years at the "Cordeillan-Bages" restaurant. With him you will discover an impressive palette of flavors united in perfect

CANNELÉS

Small rum and vanilla cake in the shape of a cylinder, the cannelé was born out the flour recuperated from the quays, first by sailors, later by nuns (late 17ᵗʰ Century) who improved it by adding milk, sugar, eggs and vanilla and who turned it into an original cake. The perfect cannelé is crunchy on top and melty on the inside. The Baillardran House improved it yet again, creating the Gold Cannelé flavored with Bourbon vanilla and flambé with rum.

harmony: *Bouillon de coquillages à la citronnelle* (lemongrass shellfish broth), four spices tuna and *foie gras, Barbue laquée à l'encre* (catfish)…

Michel Portos, two stars from the Michelin Guide, chose to *reside in* Bordeaux, in a different way; indeed you will have to cross the Garonne river to dine at the "Saint James". In addition to a faultless cuisine, sophisticated and delicate, you will enjoy a panoramic view of Bordeaux from the heights where the restaurant is situated, a few kilometers only from the city centre. There, he entirely devotes his time to a Bordelaise *terroir* inspired cuisine. *Oreille de cochon en tempura* (tempura pig ears), flamenkuche-style *foie de veau*… "La star, c'est le produit" (produce is all-important) as the Chef Bernard Loiseau used to say and Michel Portos likes to quote.

From the heights of the "Prince Noir" castle hails a legendary Bordelaise figure: Jean-Marie Amat. Light, art, volumes and the Chef's trademark cuisine: *pigeon grillé aux épices* (grilled spicy pigeon), *petite pastilla et salade d'herbes* (small pastilla [56] with fresh herb salad), *tartare de homard au caviar d'Aquitaine* (lobster tartar with Aquitaine caviar)… *Terroir* recipes with an added touch, a fabulous manner of reworking products with surprising and profoundly appropriate taste alliances.

But let us cross the stony bridge once more, back inside the city of Bordeaux

SHAD FISH

This fresh water fish can be found in the Garonne, the Gironde and the Dordogne rivers during the months of May and June. Its delicate flesh is much appreciated by Bordeaux people in spite of numerous fishbones (which disappear when cooking as the fish softens).

It is traditionally cooked in aluminum, grilled and stuffed with bay leaves, lemon and tomato slices, onion and a little sorrel. It is then seasoned with salt and pepper and topped with butter, thyme and bay leaves before being wrapped in aluminum paper.

➡ *The lamproie*

AQUITAINE CAVIAR

The Caviar de Gironde unfortunately disappeared, sturgeon fishing being forbidden since 1982 (as the species had considerably reduced). Nowadays, there exist breeding farms where recreated caviar is renowned for its great quality, capable of competing with the best wild caviars. The production is concentrated from September to January.

LAMPROIE

The lamproie, one of the oldest vertebrae on our planet, is without a doubt the dish one must taste at least once in Bordeaux! This fish, resembling a snake, starts its life in fresh waters and develops in the sea before returning to the river between the months of January and April. To cook it one must scald, grate, rinse, bleed, slice and clean it before preparing it "à la bordelaise": pan-fried leeks, young and full-bodied Bordeaux wine for the blood-bound sauce, a few sugar cubes to sweeten and long, slow cooking (mijotage).

itself, into the narrow street home of the true *Sud-Ouest* restaurant "La Tupina". Cozily seated before a welcoming fire, Jean-Pierre Xiradakis will enhance your meal with *apropos* suggestions: *Morue de Bègles* (cod from Bègles), *asperges nouvelles* (new asparagus), *esturgeon à la bordelaise* (Bordelaise-style sturgeons), *porc noir des Pyrénées* (Pyrenean Black Pork meat), *lamproie* (sea lamprey), *cassoulet* (meat and bean stew)… mouthwatering cuisine, generous and full of promises.

Bordeaux people also enjoy a little exoticism from time to time, which can be found in restaurants where foreign know-how and art is lovingly offered to the city. Make sure you pay them a visit too, nestled inside Bordelaise streets!

One of the best Chinese restaurants in France is sheltered within Bordeaux. "Au Bonheur du Palais" (Palate Bliss) – the name alone rings like a promise – offers Sichuan and Canton specialties, under the direction of Andy and Tommy Shan. *Crevettes ivraies* (shrimps), *canard des immortels* (duck), *écrevisses insolites* (crawfish), *seiches croustillantes au gingembre* (ginger crispy cuttlefish), *Coup de tonnerre aux crevettes ou au porc*… and the sharp explanations will doubtlessly enlighten you if you ask for them. These two men and their fine, sophisticated and elegant cuisine will unveil the mysteries of a country that

➡ *Preparing foie gras*

few restaurants so fitly represent. Furthermore, Hélène Yuan YUAN the sommelier's skillful wine *accords* are very much innovative. The wine cellar undoubtedly matches those of three-starred Michelin Guide restaurants...

Not far from Bordeaux city you can find the "Cordeillan-Bages" restaurant, fiefdom of the talented winegrower Jean-Michel Cazes under the management of the gifted Chef Thierry Marx, himself as much at ease in Japan as in the heart of the Médoc region! They will take you on a unique taste experimental journey and to the limits of cuisine where local produce – *saucisson* (sausage), *Blonde d'Aquitaine* (beef), *agneau de Monsieur Reyes* (lamb), *anguille* (eel) – are reworked with techniques and flavors scientifically recreated by Thierry Marx' skillful hand.

Then, from the Médoc region we go to Saint-Emilion, entering among beautiful stones and a luxuriant garden into the refined dining-room of the "L'Hostellerie De Plaisance", where Philippe Etchebest presides

Franck Descas, the "Au sarment" restaurant in Saint-Gervais

Hélène Yuan YUAN , Tommy & Andy SHAN, from the "Au bonheur du palais" restaurant

for Chantal and Gérard Perse in a spellbinding ambiance with a panoramic view of the old town. Market of the day, seasonal cuisine, selected local produce will bring onto your plate some fabulous lasagna with panfried foie gras and wild mushrooms, a great lobster half from Brittany, or again a succulent fried risotto with Thaï coconut *gelée*.

Later, take a little trip farther to Cenon, crossing the Garonne river again, to meet Nicolas Magie at "La Cape". A creative Chef, he knows how to combine regional traditional cuisine, which he masters, with innovative and surprising recipes where spices, flavors and textures harmoniously enhance one another.

And then, the sea. Rather, the *Bassin d'Arcachon*, and the *Cap-Ferret* with an astonishing view of the dune, and… Hortense. The *Cap-Ferret* would not be the same without her cuisine: *Moules frites façon Hortense* (mussels and fries), gigantic *Sole meunière,* the best fries *à l'ancienne,* small goatfish fresh from the market and, underneath the vine, the dune!

You can now enjoy all these charming and delightful places again, and when you return to your own home after having savored local delicacies, you will know that Bordeaux meets with brio the grand hopes you had placed in her before your visit. To all, *Bonnes dégustations!*

THE CHAPON FIN

This restaurant, located on rue Montesquieu near the Place des Grands-Hommes, is the oldest restaurant in Bordeaux with a very rich history. Awarded three stars by the Michelin Guide in 1933, it is also famed for its décor made of loose stones and grottos designed by the architect Cyprien-Alfred Duprat. It was patroned by famous people such as Edouard the Seventh, the Sultan of Morocco, Alphonse the Thirteenth, Sarah Bernhardt, Sacha Guitry…

➡ *Eel fricassee*

CAFÉ

➡ *The CIVB wine bar and patio*

➡ *Brigitte Lurton's Bord'eau House (play on words Bord/edge-bank, eau/water)*

Getting
around Bordeaux
some pioneers

by . Kévin . Desmond

IF EVER Jules Verne's English counterpart, H.G.Wells had chosen to park his Time Machine beneath, say, the Colonnes Rostrales de Bordeaux, he would, over the years, have enjoyed a cavalcade of the first arrivals of different types of transport to take the Bordelais to and fro, ashore and afloat.

Over the centuries, as a port, Bordeaux had often been witness to the latest technology in multiple sails, rigging and hull construction, particularly for the loading and swift delivery of wine.

This did not present other types of transport from delighting and sometimes annoying the Bordelais.

In 1765 King Louis XV allowed *sieur* Vital Muret to set up, for fifteen years, a service of 50 "carrosses de louage", or rental coaches, in Bordeaux, but also in the working class areas and suburbs.

On the morning of Wedesday 16th June 1784, three intrepid young men, Messrs Darbalet (lawyer), Degranges (wine merchant) and Chalifour (architect) made the very first aerial ascent in a Montgolfière balloon above Bordeaux. To raise money for charity, ringside spectators bought tickets, the proceeds going to a factory for poor children. Cheered by an enormous crowd, the intrepid aeronauts landed seven minutes later in the vineyard of the American consul, Mr Fenwick.

Following the French Revolution and the Napoleonic Wars, in 1818, the city saw its first paddle-steamer plying for service between Bordeaux and Langon (upstream). Aptly named *La Garonne*, it was powered by a 30hp engine built by Messrs Bolton & Watt of Birmingham, England. The patent for the paddle system was supplied by Mr Church, an American, while funds came from a

syndicate including Hugh Barton and the ubiquitous Johnston family.

1830 saw the arrival of the horse-drawn omnibus in the city – first single-decker and then double-decker. Before long some 11 private omnibus companies were circulating with names like "Les Dames Blanches" (White Ladies), "Les Favorites" and "Les Bordelaises". Eventually these were merged into the "Compagnie générale des omnibus de Bordeaux."

During the same period, Louis Godinet, a Bordeaux notary and his colleague Rocher, had been campaigning for the idea of steam railway between Bordeaux and the coastal town of La Teste. Their idea was to ultimately extend it down to Bayonne and Spain. After four years of laying railway tracks and building some 20 stations, the line was inaugurated on 6th July 1841. The train would leave Bordeaux Ségur station, on the left bank, at 4pm, only reaching La Teste the following morning, and in a carriage open to all weathers and shocks; and that only in the summer. In winter the service was reduced to transporting fish!

By 1844 there was a railway service between Bordeaux and Orléans and ten years later you could travel between Bordeaux, Angoulême and Paris, although not quite as fast as today's TGV!

In 1880 the Town Council decided to embark on the American tramway

Cycling in Bordeaux

system – still horse-drawn but along railway tracks. The 31-year concession was obtained, not by the French, but by the British Tramways & General Works Company. Within nine years, this Company was running 8 lines covering 39km – with some 120 trams (44-seaters or 38-seaters) and 137 omnibuses. A total 1,200 horses were employed, each for six hours a day.

Back on the river, over fifty steam ferryboats and barges were to be seen battling agains the strong currents of the river; they carried the delightful fleet names of *les Hirondelles* (swallows), *les Gondoles* (gondolas), *les Abeilles* (Bees) and les *Magiciennes*. This does not account for the steamships arriving from ports around the world.

Back onshore, an ever-growing numbers of bicycles and tricycles could be seen, "wheeled" by members of the

"Véloce-club Bordelais", founded in 1878. One make of cycle, made by the local gunsmith Schaudel, was called "La Bordelaise".

During 1890, Véloce Club director, Paul Legendre was seen puffing around Bordeaux in his steam-powered tricycle. Here came Bordeaux's first horseless carriage! Five years later, the town became part of the world's first timed motor trials – the Paris-Bordeaux-Paris (12,000 km) organised by the Count de Dion of the Automobile Club de France.

Inspired by the event, Paul Legendre acquired one of the very first de Dion petrol-engined tricycles, modified it and started selling copies under the name

"La Mignonette Luap". Here was the beginning of Bordeaux's automobile-building industry – with such marques as the Motobloc, built from 1902 to 1930 under the supervision of engineer Emile Dombret in the La Bastide quarter of the city.

For those not among the elite automobile owners, 1898 saw the first electric "tramway" driven by its "wattman" go into service. By 1946 the Compagnie francaise des tramways électriques et omnibus de Bordeaux – TEOB – was running some 38 lines, cover more than 200 km of track and serving 160,000 passengers.

Before long, Bordeaux also had its fleet of motor taxicabs. And from 1925, Bordeaux also had a municipal motor-bus service of 13 lines. With the popularisation of the automobile, the tramway was steadily wound down until the last rails were sent off to the scrapyard in 1958.

As for aviation, les Bordelais first applauded and cheered a heavier-than-air flying machine above the city sky on August 24th 1910. Its pilot was the famous aviator Emile Ruchonnet. But it was a local boy Marcel Issartier, flying his Deperdussin monoplane who popularised flying.

Before his premature death in 1914, Issartier not only set up Sarcignan aerodrome which became the present-day Bordeaux-Mérignac airport, but he also created Bordeaux's first flying school. During the 1920's and 1930's the aeronautics industry grew up in

the Aquitaine with the creation of SASO, and then SNCASO.

During the dark days of the 1940's the Occupied city saw its own fare share of Nazi and Italian submarines, operating from out of the indestructible Submarine Base in Bacalan.

During the early 1950's, briefly, Bordeaux had its own Grand Prix, similar to Monaco. The Bordelais cheered champions such as Albert Ascari, Juan Manuel Fangio, Giuseppe Farina, Stirling Moss and Jean Behra as they piloted their roaring Ferraris, Maseratis and Gordini's in front of the Place des Quinconces.

In 1997, the Bordeaux Urban Community decided to adopt a plan for a new tramway. By 21st December 2003, the new tram was carrying passengers on three routes. At the time of writing 43 km and 84 stations are in regular use.

The consequent reduction of automobile traffic around the city has seen the arrival of six "Bleu Line" electric buses and the return of a cycling population, including battery-electric assisted bicycles. Afloat the Construction Navale de

SOCIÉTÉ ANONYME DES
USINES MOTOBLOC
BREVETS E. DOMBRET
BORDEAUX-BASTIDE
Type O.D. No 9090 15 HP.

2 ET 3 MAI 1953

GRAND PRIX INTERNATIONAL DE VITESSE
BORDEAUX
CINZANO

Bordeaux are series-building an award-winning hybrid yacht, the *Lagoon 420*. Much of this new generation of transport owes its success to the innovative team at the IXL Electronics Laboratory of Bordeaux University.

As for the future, who knows what vehicles will delight or annoy the Bordelais? In any case, the current of the Garonne River and the steady sun of the south-west could soon be providing unlimited sources of sustainable energy for the 21st Century.

➡ *Bordeaux Quays in the Fifties*

➡ *The Town Hall at the turn of the century*

48. - BORDEAUX. - *L'Hôtel de Ville* - BR - 284

➡ *A Cruise ship on the Garonne River*

➡ *The Belem and the Aquitaine Bridge*

➡ *The Pilat Dune*

The Bassin plays a spirited water symphony of ever changing shades, of light subtle and mystifying as the sky merges into the sea.

CABANES CHANQUÉES (TYPICAL ARCACHON CABINS)

Emblematic cabins located east of Birds' Island in the Bassin d'Arcachon, they were built on concrete pillars for the most recent (1948), and wooden ones for the other (1945). One can wonder what they were used for before becoming the must-be-seen feature of the Bassin.

The importance they took in the Bordelaise collective spirit saved them, turning them into some sort of protected "species". They are now part of the maritime décor, just like the oyster-farming cabins and the pignots.

Bordeaux-upon-sea

by Charles Daney

THE BORDEAUX port was great, and busy with people from many nationalities; their longing for the sea remains. Travelling the Garonne river, a steamboat would take them to Royan, which they for a while believed to be their due property. But Royan is the Ocean. Bordeaux people like its water to be more salty than the river but as calm as the stream (such is their naming of the estuary). The ground way, then the train, brought them to the Bassin d'Arcachon. On this shore, they found what they were looking for. Those who had built great villas there contributed to the birth of a city which used to be desolated. This is why one could say that Arcachon is the Bordeaux people's city.

The Arcachon way of life was inspired by Bordeaux the earthly city. Indeed, its people could find on the "Bassin" a calm seaside, water and beach anytime and a casino, the kind of game parlor which was for a long time banned in any city other than thermal or seaside. Arcachon was to Bordeaux what Enghien was to Paris, a source of fun and "let your hair down" attitude.

Any sea carries within her froth a pinch of Anglicism, widespread by yachting on every ocean in the world.

121

➡ *The* Bassin *as seen from the* Pilat *Dune*

The solitary navigator is never lost on the Bassin...

Arcachon is not Cowes, nonetheless Philippe Jullian did venture to compare them since the bordelaise yachting club stands in between. Bordeaux is in every recess of the mind and the history of the bordelaise chronicle. The Bassin d'Arcachon would after all merely be the maritime façade of Bordeaux.

On the beach, by the sea, people are everywhere, but on the water one is blissfully alone. A breath of wind, a water murmur and everything merges into one, except on the shore where villas remain the sailor's sea marks. He knows them all, and more so when he singles his own amidst the multitude. The solitary navigator is never lost on the Bassin and, when seeking a shoal or a fairway, he never worries unduly as he is merely visiting

The Bassin d'Arcachon *with
not-to-be-missed oysters
and oysters farms*

➡ *The* Bassin d'Arcachon *Oyster Parks*

➡ *A typical fishing vessel on the* Bassin d'Arcachon *called "* La pinass*…*

his domain. However it proves rather difficult to access via the sea because of the *Passes*, and it is also quite trying to reach via land due to traffic jams. Thus, the first thing the sailor never fails to do upon his arrival in Arcachon is contemplating the water. Only then is he truly satisfied. He knows the value of happiness, and gazing at the sea is the greatest bliss of all.

The Bassin plays a spirited water symphony of ever changing shades, of light subtle and mystifying as the sky merges into the sea. There is pink in pearl, and blue, pastel colors caressed by melted silver from the sky, crossed by the setting sun's warm orange beams. Painters seek the luminosity in the Bassin because it respects the daintiest of colors.

The Arcachon casino

Coming to Arcachon is like entering one's own house, throwing its shutters wide open to waken it, bathing the bow-window with light, tidying and adding colors to the garden, happy like a puppy wagging his tail as his beloved owner returns. The ideal location is when your feet touch the water and your villa enjoys an open view of the Bassin. Nevertheless, the "winter town [57]" is the only listed district, because of an *ensemble* conception still perceivable in spite of transformations which took place over more than a century. In any way, unique details give all the villas in Arcachon, even as far the Moulleau, an indescribable air about them which only real "family" houses learnt to develop with the passing years. Their owners are so aware of this that they tirelessly return every Sunday, despite the traffic jams, to "prepare" the villa, as if they were expecting a guest.

Then, they aim for the port, the third marina in the Atlantic sea. In spite of its six hundred and fifty boat hooks, it never ceases to grow. Boats are safe there, as everyone knows, but still the view is striking, so many vessels aligned and masts hissing and grinding in the wind. No one, and especially not boat owners, would even think of missing such a sight. There is always someone to check the moors, to sweep the deck. Sailors spend a lot of

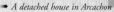 *A detached house in Arcachon*

time cleaning and washing, and any boat owner feels like a Cape Horner. All the more so there is always much to do, even in the port, especially in the port. Whether a dinghy or a ship, any boat must be ready to serve at all times, be it for the Sunday fishing trip or for leisurely sailing. Cloudy or clear, any weather is good for navigating except for storms which do not occur frequently on the Bassin, known to be an excellent and very safe navigation plan.

Navigating on the Bassin will take you on a journey full of pictorial delights, with landscapes as diverse and surprising as the shapes and shades in a kaleidoscope. Here, the islands covered in gorse, there the grassy swamps

➡ The Andernos *Pier, floodlit*

pierced with water holes sheltering hunting swamps, further on a sand border, a peaceful inlet, an "out-of-this-world" spot and still the pines as backdrop like an unfaltering open air theatre décor. Two huts stand guard on the glacis of the "île aux oiseaux [58]". Because they can be seen from nearly all angles, they leave an unforgettable mark in visitors' minds.

At the entrance, on the ocean's side and opposite the Ferret's "pointe [59]", the Pilat dune is the most beautiful sand castle one could ever dream of on the Atlantic coast; it is truly one of the world's wonders. Because it is fair,

because it is bare. The loose sand rolls and shrieks under one's steps. Winter then transforms the dune like a desert in the making: wrinkles, pyramidal shapes, crescents of sand stretching beyond the horizon. In the summer, thousands of feet tread on it without ever altering its majesty. Over one

From the top of the Pilat Dune

hundred meters of undulating hillside forever renewed as the sand dances in the wind, while the sun bathes the dune in gold as it would a yellow stone monument. At its feet, the tangle of canals and banks intertwine in an ever-changing landscape. Like a sentinel, the dune watches over the *Passes* and guides returning fishermen.

From atop the dune, beyond the Bassin and the sandbanks, Bordeaux dwellers found the ocean again… and their very reason for being there: Bordeaux-upon-Sea.

The Pilat Dune

*The story of Saint-Emilion has in fact
built itself like an adventure novel
full of twists and turns…*

Saint-Emilion

by.Stéphanie.Baudry

SAINT-EMILION IN A FEW WORDS

Saint-Emilion has always been a visitor's favourite, certainly due in part to its highly attractive location, overlooking the valley. As if we could reach the inaccessible and were about to discover something totally new. The story of Saint-Emilion has in fact built itself like an adventure novel full of twists and turns.

A LITTLE PRE-HISTORY AND HISTORY

The discovery of tools from various prehistoric times reveals the presence of man on the site at the very dawn of Humanity. It then became *terre de monastères* [60] within the first centuries of Christianism, and was given its name by a hermit who hailed from Brittany, before savage and disorderly Saracen and Normand hordes invaded it. Ravaged, the city fell into the hands of two laics, viscounts Olivier and Pierre de Castillon. The archbishops of Bordeaux Goscelin de Parthenay (in 1080) and Arnaud Guiraud (in 1100) reinstated the monastery, thus giving a religious purpose back to a city under the influence of the

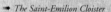
The "Ermitage"

flourishing Aquitaine episcopate.
The monastery of the *Collège des Chanoines* of Saint-Augustin and the Convent located at the top of the cliff shone with no common measure, which attracted many nomad people who helped the city prosper. Little by little, farther down the cliff side, a laic group started to develop around the old monastery of the Saint hermit Emilion. A society of enterprising and courageous men and women built houses and shops and, to protect its centre, erected surrounding walls with doors and towers out of the carriers of the city itself. Saint-Emilion was born!

The Saint-Emilion Cloister

JEAN SANS TERRE [61] AND THE CHARTE DES COMMUNES [62]

Then, in the history of Saint-Emilion, *Jean sans Terre* appeared, the brother of *Richard Cœur de Lion* [63]. When his brother died in 1199, he tried to consolidate his power by creating the *Charte des Communes*. To achieve this,

he linked to the crown a few autonomous groups of key citizens who represented the economic and military power of the country. Saint-Emilion was one of these communes! In exchange, he empowered the citizens with total freedom of lifestyle, of enterprise and customs, as well as of political or economic administration, of justice and of tax. All the liberties of an autonomous city were preserved, even that of continuing to drive its own private militia. Saint-Emilion could then become a *commune* which participated in the wealth of the medieval Aquitaine, restoring at the same time the British Crown image. One can then easily understand, as for many visitors from other countries, the interest British

tourists had in the area. Many of them even took up residence in the region. They certainly found their roots there, and felt somewhat home again!

JURADE AND JURISDICTION

The city organization followed this line of conduct for a long time, chart after chart, king after king, founded upon the Jurade system : 12 *Jurats* [64] at the head of the City, Councillors elected by the *Cent Pairs* [65], all members of the Commune. A few years later, in 1289, Edouard 1st, Duke of Guyenne, furthered the judiciary and administrative powers of the City Magistrate to the surrounding communes. A real "jurisdiction" was born, comprising nine parishes that had become communes since the Revolution. By then Saint-Emilion wines were already renowned, and the Jurade was managing the wine life and economy of the city with mastery. If in 1790, the municipality abandoned its prerogatives, in 1948, the Jurade, under a more modern form, brought its olden powers back to life by taking under its protective wing both the old

➡ *The church pillars and central nave*

The city's bell tower at nightfall

jurisdiction from the early days and the Saint-Emilion appellation.

SAINT-EMILION IN 2008

Saint-Emilion in 2008 comprises 7800 hectares, the limits of which were fixed in 1289 by the King of England Edward 1st and classified in the UNESCO World Heritage of Humanity. It is also a land of about 5000 hectares of vines lovingly tendered by men respectful of this invaluable heritage, names as prestigious as Ausone, Cheval Blanc, Angélus, Beauséjour, Canon, Figeac, Pavie, La Gaffelière, and many others. The Saint-Emilion wines entered the classification of the *Grands Crus classés* [66] in 1959. At the latest classification in 2006, 15 of them were *First Grands Crus classés*.

STROLLING THROUGH SAINT-EMILION

The Provence is not the only county to be proud of its charming villages nestled on hilltops. You will find in Saint-Emilion a little preserved village, out of time, a little off the beaten track, far from the world's agitation and in which the only *droit de cité* is walking. As you will need the use of your feet to explore it, ensure you have good walking shoes! High heels are definitely out as they certainly do not fit the old paved streets of this village which seems, besides the wall vestiges from war bombs, to sprig out of its own past. And as the pollution exhaled by our modern day toys is out of place in the village, each stone will tell you, in its own way, something of its own history. Each tiny street running back up an impressive slope, glimpsed from the corner of your eye as

The underground wine storehouses of the Ausone Castle

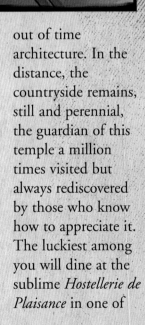

you stop to catch your breath again, will whisper in your ear a piece of the past brought back into present time reality. And if the stones remain quiet, it will be a wine merchant or a restaurant owner, a *cafetier* who will recount one of the innumerable Catacombs stories, thus telling you what you ignored still about wine and how to enjoy it. Because, if there indeed is a Temple of Wine, it has been edified in Saint-Emilion! Bottles aligned with care, methodically, near-monastically from the house of wines and wine merchants, with innovative cork-screws, decanters and magical utensils to prevent vermillion drops from falling on your perfectly white napkin: you will find every secret that wine and its commerce can reveal. After getting lost in a maze of boutiques, art galleries, cafés and restaurants, after admiring the subtle mixture of elegantly arranged stones and flowery plants, take a rest for a moment against the parapet and contemplate, beyond the rooftops, the vestiges of an out of time architecture. In the distance, the countryside remains, still and perennial, the guardian of this temple a million times visited but always rediscovered by those who know how to appreciate it. The luckiest among you will dine at the sublime *Hostellerie de Plaisance* in one of

➡ *The Ausone Castle under the mist*

its many hillside dining areas. The stone restaurant *Etchebest* will take you into the temple of French gastronomy, an alert and forever evolving temple to keep your taste buds enthralled. The cave, majestic epitome of the city, mysterious receptacle, will not deceive you either. A room perfect in decoration and refinement will then complete the journey, already full of unforgettable memories. Upon awakening, you will find yourself overlooking the sleepy city in the divine vision of a morning where the light will soon flood the Bordeaux stones, light and soft, before your eyes. And if you do not have such luck, you will still have what is most precious: the desire to come back, often, and to make your friends discover this incomparable city, our very own bordelaise "Venice".

The Collegiale Cloister in Saint-Emilion

Notes

[1] Bordeaux Wines (tn)

[2] "Appellation d'Origine Contrôlée" or "Controlled Appellation of Origin" (tn)

[3] Great First Vintages (tn)

[4] This expression refers to the pointy ends of pebbles (grave as in graviers) in the area (tn)

[5] The Black Prince (tn)

[6] Ranked (tn)

[7] Ranked First Great Vintage (tn)

[8] Art of living (tn)

[9] Grape variety (tn)

[10] An amphitheater which could accommodate 15,000 spectators (the only relic of ancient Burdigala) (tn)

[11] The Big Bell (tn)

[12] "The great Intendants" (tn)

[13] Original French phrase : "La forme d'une ville / Change plus vite hélas, que le cœur d'un mortel…" (tn)

[14] *"Je suis né à Burdigala où le ciel est doux et clément, le printemps long et l'hiver bref, les collines boisées. Son fleuve bouillonne, imitant le reflux des mers… J'admire la belle ordonnance des demeures, les vastes places, les portiques ouverts au bout des rues… Salut, fontaine à la source inconnue, sainte, éternelle, cristalline, murmurante, limpide, ombragée. Salut, génie de la ville, fontaine appelée Divona, dans la langue des Celtes et mise au rang des Divinités… De Rome et Burdigala, laquelle l'emporte ? Burdigala a mon amour, Rome ma vénération. Ici est mon berceau, là ma chaise curule"*

[15] A large Roman necropolis (tn)

[16] First magistrate (tn)

[17] A kind of "heavy artillery president" (tn)

[18] "The Spirit of the Laws", 1748 (tn)

[19] "Spirit of the laws street" (tn)

[20] "Distressing dawn" (tn)

[21] "The houses, the streets of Bordeaux represent my entire youth as now detached from me" (tn)

[22] "Bordeaux the Great" (tn)

[23] "To be allowed to reside" (tn)

[24] The god of wine in Greek Mythology (tn)

[25] "Castles", "beautiful" (tn)

[26] "Que c'est beau", literally : "it is so beautiful" in French SMS language (tn)

[27] Point of Sale

[28] Play on words based on the French "Liberté Egalité Fraternité" (tn)

[29] "The Characters' House" (tn)

[30] Supplications (tn)

[31] Wish to see men free from prejudgments (tn)

[32] "As seen from the Chartrons quay" (tn)

[33] "Tramway by the Quinconces on a rainy day" (tn)

[34] "The Bordeaux port as seen from the Queries quay" (tn)

[35] "The Bordeaux port" (tn)

[36] *The Glory of Bordeaux" (tn)*

[37] "The Grand Theatre and the beginning of the Tourny Alleys" (tn)

[38] "The Bordeaux Bulls" (tn)

[39] "The Bordeaux Milkwoman" (tn)

[40] "Gallien Palace" (tn)

[41] "As seen from the Gallien Palace" (tn)

[42] "Public Garden" (tn)

[43] "The Horse Fair" (tn)

[44] Ladies of the night (tn)

[45] "I saw that" (tn)

[46] The Peyrelebade Estate" (tn)

[47] "The small boats" (tn)

[48] "Blacks" (tn)

[49] From the Médoc region (tn)

[50] A broader movement for crafts ranging from mechanics to shoemaking to gardening (tn)

[51] Security guard delivering money (tn)

[52] The Certificat d'Aptitude Professionnelle (CAP) or the Brevet d'Enseignement Professionnel (BEP) can both lead to a Baccalauréat Professionel, which in turn leads into the world of work (tn)

[53] A sort of "external candidate", term used by the French when sitting an exam having not attended classes (tn)

[54] Beef carrot, Lamb from Pauillac, Sausage from the Médoc region, Chicken broth (tn)

[55] Veal sweetbreads (tn)

[56] Sweet and savory flaky pastry filled with a subtle mixture of sautéed chicken, onions, candied lemon, pink olives, garlic, prunes and Middle Eastern spices with scrambled eggs and phyllo dusted with cinnamon sugar. (tn)

[57] An area of Arcachon

[58] Bird's island (tn)

[59] Peak point (tn)

[60] Land of monasteries (tn)

[61] John Lackland (tn)

[62] Communal Charter (tn)

[63] Richard the Lionheart (tn)

[64] "A sworn officer ; a magistrate ; a member of a permanent jury" (tn)

[65] Hundred Peers (tn)

[66] Classified Grands Crus (tn)